Praise for **The Mindful Child**

"Susan Kaiser Greenland has created unique and effective everyday practices that can be used by educators and parents alike to provide enjoyable experiences for children and teens that cultivate resourcefulness, focus, and resilience. Readers will be captivated by the inspiring examples from real-life experiences that stimulate the imagination and inspire us to awaken our lives to the power of mindfulness as a health-promoting, stress-reducing, and compassion-generating way of being."

—Daniel J. Siegel, M.D., codirector,
UCLA Mindful Awareness Research Center,
executive director, Mindsight Institute,
and author of *Mindsight* and *The Mindful Brain*

"Susan Kaiser Greenland is the real thing. She is not just teaching young children how to focus their attention more effectively, the secret to how to control their own brains; she is teaching children how to become wise, way before most kids generally understand the value of wisdom. This is a most important book; any parent who cares about raising good, morally responsible children must read it."

—Jeffrey Schwartz, author of *The Mind and the Brain*
(with Sharon Begley)

"Parents often ask me for advice about being mindful with their children. From here on out, I will refer them to this tremendously helpful book, filled with clear insights about children and how to teach them gently and skillfully. A truly inspiring book."

—Sharon Salzberg, author of *Lovingkindness:*
The Revolutionary Art of Happiness

"What a wonderful and timely antidote to the hyperactive culture that makes kids super-wired but too disconnected from themselves and others. Every parent should read *The Mindful Child* for practical strategies to teach boys and girls how to manage stress and pay attention to what really matters."

—David Walsh, Ph.D., author of
Why Do They Act That Way? A Survival Guide to the Adolescent Brain for You and Your Teen, and *No. Why Kids—of All Ages—Need to Hear It and Ways Parents Can Say It*

"There are all sorts of great books about helping children by improving parenting skills and communications—things outside the child's skin. *The Mindful Child* is a different kind of book! Readers will envision themselves *being* more effective with children rather than *working* with them. Susan Kaiser Greenland emphasizes *directly* changing the inside rather than encouraging the inside change from all that seeps in from the outside. This unique author delves into the heart of developing character and coping skills that enable children to resolutely and effectively handle difficult situations through a more relaxed self-awareness."

—Foster Cline, author of *Parenting with Love and Logic*

"In her delightful book, Susan offers parents an alternative to materialist culture by cultivating attention, emotional balance, and compassion. Filled with engaging stories and playful activities, her dedication to making classical themes accessible to all children is evident throughout."

—B. Alan Wallace, president, Santa Barbara Institute for Consciousness Studies, and author of *Mind in Balance* and *The Attention Revolution*

"In this lovely book, Susan Kaiser Greenland gives parents practical ways to keep alive curiosity, compassion, and the timeless nature of childhood when raising children in the high-tech, frantic pace of life in the twenty-first century."

—Susan L. Smalley, Ph.D., professor, Department of Psychiatry, UCLA, founder and director, Mindful Awareness Research Center, Semel Institute of Neuroscience and Human Behavior

"Mindfulness is not a luxury, it is at the heart of our lives. Susan Kaiser Greenland brilliantly demonstrates how mindfulness can give a child a major tool to flourish throughout his life."

—Matthieu Ricard, author of *Happiness: A Guide to Developing Life's Most Important Skill*

The Mindful Child

The Mindful Child

How to Help Your Kid
Manage Stress and
Become Happier, Kinder,
and More Compassionate

Susan Kaiser Greenland

ATRIA PAPERBACK

NEW YORK   LONDON   TORONTO   SYDNEY   NEW DELHI

ATRIA PAPERBACK
A Division of Simon & Schuster, Inc.
1230 Avenue of the Americas
New York, NY 10020

First Atria Paperback edition April 2013

ATRIA PAPERBACK and colophon are trademarks of Simon & Schuster, Inc.

For information about special discounts for bulk purchases, please contact Simon & Schuster Special Sales at 1-866-506-1949 or business@simonandschuster.com.

The Simon & Schuster Speakers Bureau can bring authors to your live event. For more information or to book an event contact the Simon & Schuster Speakers Bureau at 1-866-248-3049 or visit our website at www.simonspeakers.com.

Designed by Mspace/Maura Fadden Rosenthal

Manufactured in the United States of America

20   19   18   17   16   15   14   13   12   11

The Library of Congress has cataloged the Free Press edition as follows:

Greenland, Susan Kaiser.
    The mindful child : how to help your kid manage stress and become happier, kinder, and more compassionate / Susan Kaiser Greenland.
        p. cm.
    Includes bibliographical references and index.
    1. Stress management for children.   2. Child rearing.   3. Parenting.
I. Title.
    BF723.S75G74 2010
    649'.6—dc22   2009041450

ISBN 978-1-4165-8300-4
ISBN 978-1-4165-8356-1 (ebook)

To Seth
For Seeing Me

Contents

CONTENTS

The Mindful Child

The New ABCs:

Attention, Balance,

and Compassion

May the world be happy
May the world be clean
May the world never end
May the world be this way
May everything come true

> *Friendly wishes poem by Inner Kids*
> *elementary school student*

After my son's sixth birthday party, I watched from the kitchen window as the few remaining children played in the backyard. The girl from next door was doing cartwheels across our lawn, which was littered with deflated balloons. My son and his friend sat on the steps and paged through a book of cartoons he had received as a present. It was a wonderful, peaceful afternoon.

Suddenly, the calm broke: the kitchen door flew open, and my son and his friend ran in, both boys near tears. I asked them what was wrong, but they were overexcited and couldn't get the words out. No one was in danger, but the boys had worked themselves into such a state that they couldn't calm down. So I took a snow

globe from the bookshelf and wound up the music box at its base.
I shook the snow globe, put it down on a table, put my hand on my
abdomen, and asked the boys to put their hands on their tummies.
Together we felt our breaths move up and down as we watched the
snow fall and settle in the globe. My son's friend was almost gasping
as he tried to hold back his tears. When the snow had settled to the
bottom of the snow globe, I shook it again. As we watched the
water in the globe gradually clear, we felt ourselves breathing. Soon,
we could see the figures inside the snow globe and the boys' breathing had slowed; their bodies had relaxed and calmed. Now we could
talk about what had scared them.

I use this breathing technique and ones like it to help children
calm themselves when they feel overwhelmed, and the transformative power of breathing never ceases to amaze me. Breathing is the
most natural thing in the world, the foundation of our lives. We do
it without thinking about it, but by tapping into the power of this
simple act, we can better manage stress and live happier lives. The
aim of this book is to help you help your children do just that: to
tap into their awareness of breathing, the physical world, and their
inner lives, and to develop their attention skills—tools that they
will carry with them through their entire lives.

You can learn a lot by paying attention to your children's breathing. When my first child, Allegra, was born, I became more attuned
to the breathing of those around me. The first time I held her, I
watched her breathe for a while, and each breath reassured me that
she would be all right. My son, Gabe, was born two and a half years
later, and hearing the steady in and out of his breathing was as reassuring to me as the sound of his sister's breathing. Allegra and
Gabe's breathing would always be their companions, and they
would become mine. I took what I had learned from my children
into other relationships, too. I began to sit with family members
who seemed helpless due to youth, old age, or illness, and I listened
for the sound of their breathing, hearing in each breath a promise
that we would spend another day together. Years later I would look
back and recognize these moments as ones of mindful awareness, a
powerful practice that I later studied formally.

Your children's breathing is the swinging door between their inner and outer worlds. Most of us know intuitively that tuning into our own breath is useful, but we can forget that paying attention to other people's breathing can let us know how they are reacting to life experience. If you take the time to be observant, the speed, depth, pace, and intensity of your children's breathing will convey how they feel and even signal possible health issues. Your children's breathing can give you a glimpse of their lives from the inside out. You can become more mindful through simple acts, such as taking a moment in your children's bedroom to watch them peacefully and breathe with them before you wake them for school. You can observe your spouse's or partner's breathing to get a sense of what he or she is experiencing and better synchronize your pace with his or hers. You can connect deeply with an aging or ill parent by putting aside any thoughts or emotions that might be on your mind for just a moment to tune in to his or her breathing. By slowing down simply to notice other people's breathing, you can gain insights into their worlds that you might otherwise miss. And you may also gain insights into your own.

Your children's breathing is not only a message from their inner worlds. It tells you about their outer world as well—for example, their relationship with you, with siblings, with authority figures, with peers, and with the social world in general. You can especially see this in action when they interact with friends. I learned a lot about my daughter by observing her as she rows with her crew team. Each spring, her team competes in regattas throughout California. The intense physicality and concentration of the athletes as they synchronize their strokes is stunning. Their breath powers the boat. One breath, one stroke, with a laserlike focus that is fueled by years of training and the sweat of many, many races. Each stroke calls for focus on the present moment (what's happening right now), wisdom gleaned from other races (past experience), and determination to put every bit of their effort toward a common goal (the drive to win the race). When racing well, the rowers are completely attuned to one another, and the alert, visceral, and interconnected way they work together is an example of relational mindful awareness.

My first formal experience with mindfulness meditation was in 1993, when Allegra was two years old and I was three months pregnant with Gabe. We lived in New York City, and I was an in-house lawyer for ABC Television, with a happy family life, meaningful friendships, and a progressive job-sharing arrangement that allowed me to spend time at home with my toddler. Life was good. It was mind-bogglingly good, until we got a message from the internist that my husband, Seth, had stage-four lymphoma. Our lives changed in an instant.

We needed to make sense of what had happened and manage the stress that lay ahead. We read books and spoke to friends. Ultimately, Seth brought me to the Zen Center to manage my worry through meditation (the irony is not lost on me that although he had the cancer diagnosis, he took *me* to learn meditation). After an orientation meeting, we sat cross-legged on buckwheat-filled meditation cushions, faced a blank white wall, and began the process of mindfulness training. In the eerie quiet, my thoughts were deafening. I could not sit still.

Seth started chemotherapy, I quit my job, and we moved from Manhattan to a rented house in upstate New York. We hoped the slower pace of life would help Seth beat cancer, and it did. We ate organic food when we could get it. Gabe was born, Seth became involved in a radical course of alternative cancer therapy, and I tried meditation again.

Through recordings by meditation teachers Jack Kornfield and Joseph Goldstein, I learned of a Buddhist meditation practice known as mindfulness of breathing.[1] The classical instruction for this type of meditation is:

> . . . having gone to the forest, to the foot of a tree or to an empty hut, [you] sit down, folding [your] legs crosswise, holding [your] body erect, setting up mindfulness in front of [you]. Ever mindful [you] breathe in, mindful [you] breathe out.[2]

For parents, even the first step—find a quiet place with few distractions—can be challenging. But with some ingenuity, it is possible for parents to find time to meditate, which is the foundation of mindfulness practice.

One of my favorite words from classical mindfulness teachings is *householder,* which means "layperson" and is used to distinguish those who meditate but have not taken monastic vows from Buddhist monks. The word *householder* aptly reflects the life of a parent who juggles myriad, often competing, responsibilities and every day proves the truth in the saying, "If you need to get something done, ask a busy person to do it." Somehow, they manage kids, jobs, and community obligations, and they still attend parent meetings at their kids' schools, serve hot lunches, coach sports teams, sew costumes, and drive car pools. Parents have such busy lives that it might seem impossible to find a quiet place to meditate even for a short period of time. But no matter how many children and how many responsibilities we have, there's room in our schedules to meditate—we'll just have to be creative about figuring out when and where. Parents meditate at strange times and in strange places: on a cushion in their bedrooms first thing in the morning, at the kitchen table while their children are napping, in the car pool lines and while walking the halls of hospitals and retirement homes. We grab whatever time is available to us, wherever and whenever we can. We meditate when we're sitting, when we're walking, and when we're lying down, so that we can take the mindfulness developed during formal meditation into our daily lives. It's tough, but we can find pockets of time.

The next step in mindful breathing is: "setting up mindfulness in front of [you] . . . ever mindful [you] breathe in, mindful [you] breathe out." The phrase "ever mindful" can be confusing, especially since there are several different connotations for the word *mindful* now that meditation has entered secular culture. But here's a *classical* description of mindfulness that those new to meditation often find helpful: *Mindfulness is a mirror of what's happening in the present moment.*

In other words, when practicing mindfulness, you see life

experience clearly, as it happens, without an emotional charge. We learn how to do this by feeling our present moment experience, as it happens, without analyzing it—at least for the time being. To notice something and *not* analyze or think about what it means is a radical idea for many of us. It requires quieting your thoughts, emotions, and reactions—keeping your mind out of the way—so that you can take in information from your inner and outer worlds and see it clearly without the filter of preconceived notions. And you can achieve this seemingly impossible task simply by focusing on your breathing.

> *Keep your mind on the feeling of your breath as it moves from the tip of your nostrils into your chest and back out again. If your mind wanders, which it usually does, that's okay. When you see that it's wandered, bring it back to the feeling of the movement of your breath. Breathe in, breathe out. Let everything else drop away for the length of one breath and feel what it's like to be alive right now, in the present moment.*

This and other meditation techniques like it have been practiced for thousands of years by all major religions and contemplative traditions. These practices systematically develop attention while encouraging kindness, compassion, and self-knowledge. Mindful awareness promotes physical and mental well-being as well as character and ethical development, a claim supported by growing data from major universities around the world. Many people find that it just makes them happier. Mindfulness practice helped me recognize unhealthy patterns of thinking and reacting to life experience without judging myself harshly. It also showed me the way to a joyful and transcendent state of well-being that I had previously stumbled upon but didn't know how to access intentionally until I learned to meditate.

Once I saw its benefits in my own life, I wondered if mindfulness would help my children. How much richer might their childhoods be if they could use age-appropriate mindful awareness techniques? I soon discovered, however, that while there were hundreds of places where adults could receive secular training, as well as many good books they could read, there were no secular programs or books about teaching mindfulness to children at the time.[3] It occurred to me that perhaps I could adapt the mindfulness techniques I practiced to make them appropriate for my family.

I began developing simple practices and teaching them to Gabe and Allegra. There was absolutely nothing scientific about what I was doing, but the kids were interested, and I soon sensed a change in them. Had you asked them if they were practicing mindfulness, they would have denied it, but they nonetheless used breath awareness to help them slow down when they were overexcited and become calmer when they were upset. Both children were less reactive to big and small irritants than they had been before. Something was working, so I became a bit more daring. I met with the director of the Boys and Girls Club in Santa Monica, California, in the fall of 2000 and offered to volunteer two hours a week to teach in their after-school day-care program. While the director was initially reluctant (and no wonder, given that I had no scientific credentials at the time), he agreed, and I began improvising classes in the art room. My friend, Dr. Suzi Tortora, a dance therapist who teaches children breath awareness and movement, visited from New York and helped me incorporate mindful movement into the classes. During that period, I developed many of the core practices I teach today.

In 2001, another friend, Steve Reidman, a public school teacher in Los Angeles, heard what I was doing and asked me to work with his students. He had a particularly rambunctious class and was looking for any outside help to manage it. Reidman's students embraced the program, and to everyone's surprise, some of the kids even began taking the practices home and teaching them to their parents. My favorite story from that year, one that has since been repeated many times by parents of children from different cities, was shared by the mother of a ten-year-old girl. She described driving her children to school during morning rush hour when traffic had come to a standstill. The mom became understandably frustrated, honking at other cars and frenetically trying to find a traffic report on the radio when, out of the backseat, a little voice said, "Mom, just take three deep breaths; it will calm you down." The woman took her daughter's advice, and the tension eased. It didn't stop them from being late, but they arrived at their destination considerably less frazzled than usual. That day, mindful awareness had a new convert in the parent body of the school.

Support for the program continued to build, and by the end of the first year, students, teachers, parents, and administrators all considered the project a success. Significantly, the general atmosphere in the classroom had improved, and Reidman attributed that improvement, at least in part, to mindfulness. I returned to Reidman's class the following year, and slowly, through word of mouth, teachers and administrators at other schools asked me to teach.

Teaching mindful awareness in schools is deeply gratifying and has the potential to make a large-scale, positive impact on our society. This benefit, however, while great, is different from the benefit that accrues to kids when their entire family system practices mindful awareness. The more I worked with schools, the more I recognized the inherent limitations in working with children outside of the family system. Psychotherapist and meditation teacher Trudy Goodman and I started a small family program in my backyard in order to work directly with parents and their children.

Most parents who come to me hope that their children grow up to be people who, even during the most stressful or provocative situations, choose to give themselves enough time to develop a perspective that will help them make sound, productive decisions. They want their children to live happier lives. Some of these parents are looking to mindfulness as a spiritual practice, but most of them are not. They want to help their children develop life skills, like how to:

- Approach experience with curiosity and an open mind
- Calm down when they're angry or upset
- Concentrate and ignore distractions
- See what's happening in, to, and around them, other people, and the environment clearly and objectively
- Develop compassion
- Develop prosocial qualities like patience, humility, happiness for the good fortune of others, generosity, diligence, and equanimity
- Live gently and in balance with other people and their environment.

Some young people have a hard time learning and applying these life skills, but most are well able to practice mindful awareness when they receive clear and concrete instruction and live in an environment supportive of the process. This is especially true when the practices are fun, and kids begin to see for themselves how mindfulness can help them navigate even the most challenging real-life situations. This book will show how you and your children can develop these hugely beneficial skills in your own home.

I was inspired to write this book by the parents who reached out because their children had problems that they hoped mindfulness training could help. One child was friendless, for example, and the parents could not understand why. Another was starting fights in school, and his parents were afraid that the school would expel him or, worse, that he would seriously hurt another child or himself. A third child had trouble sleeping and often awoke in the middle of the night and began to cry, not knowing why or how to stop. A fourth child was in frequent pain due to illness, made worse by tension in her mind and body. Another seemed to be a model child, except that she put so much pressure on herself she collapsed whenever she experienced anything less than perfection. The parents of these children felt desperate and were willing to give anything a try if there was a remote possibility it could help.

The children whose stories are told throughout the book are composites of children with whom I've worked. No real names or identifying details are used. Let's start with Nick, Melody, and Charlotte.

Nick, a sixth grader referred to me by his physician, complained of being unhappy, truly unhappy, and over time he had developed sleep and digestive problems. His doctor was quite sure that no underlying medical disorder could account for Nick's sadness, although both his physician and parents accepted that his problems were serious and he needed help. By the time I met Nick, his schoolwork was suffering, as was his social life. When his mom picked him up from school, Nick often burst into tears, saying that he hated his life, his friends, everything and everyone but his family.

I spoke with Nick about why he was unhappy. He told me he couldn't put his finger on anything in particular that was wrong, but he couldn't put his negative thoughts aside. Like many adults, he had never considered the possibility that a person could influence how he reacted to his thoughts and emotions. Nick believed that thoughts, positive as well as negative, just came into your head uninvited and that there was little if anything you could do about it.

Melody had been diagnosed with ADHD. When I first met her, she had difficulty looking at me, and she blurted out immediate, and mostly unconsidered, responses to everything I said, regardless of whether my statement called for a response. I guessed that this was the same way she interacted with her teachers and friends. Teachers are trained to understand this behavior, but other children greeted her impulsivity with rolling eyes and sniggers. It wasn't that her remarks were stupid. They were often insightful and clever. But she tended to offer them with much more enthusiasm than the situation called for, and with no sense of the pace or intensity of the conversation. Melody had few friends and was not invited to play dates, the movies, or classmates' birthday parties.

Charlotte, a high school junior, was referred to me for chronic, debilitating headaches. Charlotte was in the middle of an intense headache when she first came to see me. As her mom and I spoke, Charlotte moved to a corner of the room, listening to her iPod and drawing on a dry-erase board. Charlotte's mom noticed what she was doing, and called out, "Charlotte, don't push yourself right now; it will just make your headache worse." I was dumbstruck when I realized that Charlotte was powering through her headache, listening to Mandarin Chinese language tapes on her iPod and writing sentences on the board in Mandarin.

Neither Charlotte nor anyone in her family was Chinese. Charlotte was learning Mandarin because she hoped that foreign language fluency would look good on her college application. Her mother had done everything she could to convince her daughter to give herself a break, but nothing had worked. Charlotte persisted in believing that in everything she attempted, there were only two options: absolute perfection and abject failure.

These children were smart people who had somehow locked themselves into an exhausting, downbeat way of seeing the world and relating to life experience. Mindful awareness can help children like Nick, Melody, and Charlotte shift their negative conceptual framework to a more positive one. Changing the way you think about things and react to life events takes hard work, practice, strong modeling, and guidance. But with appropriate effort, a supportive environment, and a bit of luck, the process will take hold and then change will happen naturally. The first step in this process is learning to recognize what your conceptual framework is then, if necessary, working toward dismantling it in order to get a more accurate read on what's happening in, to, and around you. That's where mindful awareness practice can be quite helpful to those who are developmentally ready.

Twenty-five hundred years ago, Aristotle observed that "we are what we repeatedly do," and the same holds true now. What we think, say, and do today will influence what we think, say, and do tomorrow. It's easy to develop habitual patterns of speech, behavior, and thought without realizing it. Mindfulness of breathing, when practiced properly, helps develop a stable and strong faculty of attention capable of recognizing these patterns. You must see whether or not you have biases or patterns of behavior that you'd like to shift before you can change them.

By practicing mindfulness kids learn life skills that help them soothe and calm themselves, bring awareness to their inner and outer experience, and bring a reflective quality to their actions and relationships. Living in this way helps children connect to themselves (what do I feel? think? see?), to others (what do they feel? think? see?), and maybe to something greater than themselves. This is a worldview in which everything is seen as interconnected. When children understand that they and those they love are somehow connected to everybody and everything else, ethical and socially productive behavior comes naturally, and they also feel less isolated—a common problem for kids and teens. In a world where the most popular reality television shows involve harsh criticism and ridicule of the contestants, it is no wonder that children often make light of old-fashioned values like kindness, compassion, and gratitude. But in mindfulness practice, these qualities are prized above all. And because children learn to be aware of the impact of their actions and words on others, they consider other people when setting goals and planning, and they are more likely to be kind to themselves, too, during moments of real or perceived failure.

A common misconception about mindfulness is that it is exclusively about sitting quietly and meditating. But that couldn't be further from the truth. Introspection is a critical element in understanding life experience in a clear and unbiased way, but what good is that skill if children can't use it in real-life situations? The skills of mindfulness find their highest value as children navigate the world every day, during which they give children and teens a road map to plan, organize, and think through complex problems. It helps them define what they want (or need) to do and set forth making a plan to accomplish it.

Chapters 1 Through 4:
The Building Blocks of Mindfulness

Mindfulness practice is serious work with important, long-term implications for overall health and well-being, but above all, it is a pleasure and can be presented playfully and effectively. In Chapters 1 through 4, I will share activities and exercises through which parents and children can learn mindfulness-based calming techniques and develop strong and stable attention skills—the building blocks of mindfulness. Chapter 1 will focus on the science and theory behind mindfulness, including ways to explain mindfulness to children. Since it's easy to take mindfulness, especially attention training, a little too seriously and forget that fun, in and of itself, is healing, useful, and productive, Chapters 2 through 4 are full of games, songs, pictures, and poems that I've found to be effective in developing the mindfulness skills. For example, when a young child is upset or there is family conflict, you can sing a song about breathing together, or she can calm herself by putting a stuffed animal on her stomach and pretending to rock it to sleep. Playing mindfulness-related games and singing mindfulness-related songs are fun ways to help children develop attention skills and understand how breath awareness can help them self-regulate. It's also a great way to jump-start a period of introspection.

One of the biggest challenges for those who meditate is to put thoughts aside and rest in their present-moment experience. We think most of the time, and putting it aside can be difficult. But when we're having fun, we tend to put thinking aside automatically. Playing games and singing helps kids (and adults) break free of their conceptual framework, and these activities are a fantastic prelude to practicing meditation. As a practical matter, it tends to be easier for newcomers to stop thinking naturally, through play, before they meditate than to stop thinking deliberately after they sit down on a cushion.

If you are wondering, But how do I get my son or daughter to do this? Here's what I suggest to beginners:

Concentrate on the feeling of your breath as it moves through your body. If your mind wanders, that's perfectly natural; just bring it back to the physical sensation of your inhalation, your exhalation, and the pause between the two. Remember, don't think about your breathing or change it in any way, just feel your breath as it is right now and rest.

Chapters 5 and 6:
Clearly Seeing and Understanding
Life Experience

In Chapters 5 and 6, I encourage children and teens to use their attention skills and breath awareness to help them better understand what's happening in, to, and around them. When they notice mental and physical discomfort, I invite children to pretend they are scientists studying a rare species (themselves!) by feeling what happens to their minds and bodies in response. They use their innate curiosity to understand better the discomfort, and at first, all they do is feel it. Does it change or stay the same? Does it move or stay in one place? Is there a connection between things they do or say and how they feel? Is there a connection between how they feel and the things they do or say? Often physical and mental discomfort will ease simply because part of them is experiencing it with the eye of a curious but dispassionate scientist. Dr. Jeffrey Schwartz, from the University of California, Los Angeles, describes this nonreactive, scientific perspective as that of an impartial spectator. When working with children, I emphasize that this perspective is also clear-headed and compassionate. I don't ask kids to ignore unpleasant realities, but to recognize that there may be a lot they don't know about people and situations that seem difficult or unfair.

The story *Beauty and the Beast* helps kids understand that things are not always what they appear to be. Beast is horrible at the beginning of the story, but over time Beauty sees a kinder Beast underneath his frightening exterior. The ultimate revelation comes when Beauty learns that a cruel spell has locked a prince in Beast's body all this time, and only her choice to marry him could unlock the prince. Beauty realizes that she cannot judge a person on appearances alone—in other words, no wonder Beast was so cranky before! Mindfulness practice helps kids see beyond the surface of the beasts in their own lives by learning to approach them with an open mind, curiosity, and compassion.

Once kids learn to stabilize their attention, the emphasis shifts to watching inner experience (thoughts, emotions, and physical sensations) without analyzing it—in other words, without labeling the experience as good or bad. For example, Melody noticed she had a habit of wanting to answer every single question regardless of what it was. She didn't judge the habit as good or bad. She just looked at it and paid attention to how she felt when she wasn't called on. I encouraged Melody to notice how she felt every time she wanted to answer a question, paying attention to the sensations in her body. Melody's actions and reactions would evolve over time, but first, she had to make a connection between what was happening in her mind, in her body, and in her behavior.

Nick, Melody, and Charlotte all saw connections between their feelings and different aspects of their lives. Nick was able to see that his loneliness and boredom were connected to his feelings of sadness, and Charlotte recognized that working hard didn't always make her feel better about herself—in fact, it sometimes made her feel worse because stress triggered her chronic headaches. Nick and Charlotte made these observations without the emotional sting of judgment. All three children opened up to their parents more and talked about their worries, fears, goals, and aspirations.

Chapters 8 and 9:
Using Mindfulness in Real Life

In Chapters 8 and 9, children and teens use what they learn while practicing mindfulness to understand better the outside world and how they choose to live in it. By paying close attention to what they do throughout the day, children and teens can discover their own habits of mind (for example, procrastination, optimism, or pessimism), and of their bodies (for example, whether they are active or sedentary). Children can then better recognize how these habits affect their lives and better understand that some habits, like kindness, will more likely lead to happiness than others.

Nick realized that he tended not to choose what he wanted to do, but instead relied on his parents to choose for him. Nick recognized that he didn't choose his friends, either, but hung out with whoever was available. He decided to focus on what he liked to do and finding friends who shared his interests. Melody realized that raising her hand every time a teacher asked a question (even when she wasn't sure of the answer) was only a habit. Her classroom teacher and her parents encouraged Melody to raise her hand more deliberately. The teacher reinforced Melody's self-regulatory behavior by calling on her quickly, knowing that Melody would have thought through her answer before raising her hand. Melody became more reflective as she learned to raise her hand intentionally rather than automatically. Charlotte realized that her compulsion to work was a habit. Without thinking, she worked whenever she had the chance. Once she realized that she was working automatically, rather than deliberately, she started to consider how she wanted to spend her time. She loved jazz and hoped to excel at jazz flute, so she decided to spend more time listening to jazz and practicing the flute, rather than busying herself in work that was unnecessary.

By slowing down to feel what's happening in their inner and outer worlds objectively and with compassion, and then acting mindfully, Nick, Melody, and Charlotte recognized that they were not helpless victims of their own automatic thought processes, and that they could control how they responded to situations even if they couldn't control the situation itself. After Nick discovered more fulfilling interests and friendships, he also became more resilient and noticed to his great relief that his parents relaxed.

Even though Melody was only in elementary school, she began to see a connection between her over-the-top enthusiasm and her classmates' withdrawal from her. Slowly, she began to spot when she lost control of her actions and was often able to calm herself with breath awareness. Soon she found herself picking up on social cues she had missed before, and more important, she no longer had to try so hard to win acceptance. Before long, she found other friends who were similarly enthusiastic and whose approval she did not need to win.

Charlotte decided not to spread herself too thin and found that applying herself selectively made her more likely to excel in those one or two areas on which she chose to focus—the very thing she was told college counselors were looking for in a candidate. By freeing herself from the tyranny created by her need to be the best at everything she did, she became happier and more comfortable relaxing with friends and family. She started to go out with friends more often and have some fun. It was not surprising that her headaches became less frequent and debilitating.

Through the practice of mindfulness, Nick, Melody, and Charlotte began to see their lives through a different lens. They became less self-involved and more connected to others. Many mindfulness students find this to be the case. For example, a high school student wrote: "With mindfulness, I realized that not everything revolves around me. I knew that before, but now it is much easier for me to know that I can be who I am but not the center of the world." Great thinkers, scientists, statesmen, artists, teachers, parents, and other outstanding citizens share this insight, and it is a perspective that we all need in order to think creatively in our complex and ever-changing world.

The New ABCs:
Attention, Balance, and Compassion

Every movement has its breakthrough moment when it no longer has to defend its message. Mindful awareness training for children has arrived at that moment. By joining a more reflective and introspective way of being with the insights from modern psychology and neuroscience, we can refine how we teach our children. The traditional ABCs of reading, writing, and arithmetic that served us well for generations don't serve us fully anymore. Helping kids build strong academic skills is fantastic, but that's just one of many elements that make a well-rounded education. We've seen children do well academically but struggle socially and suffer emotionally. We've seen the toll stress has taken on the health and well-being of many kids. In response, the focus of education has broadened beyond academics to serve the whole child. The aim of secular mindfulness training is for children and teens to learn academic, social, and emotional skills in a balanced way. Classical mindfulness practice focuses on the cultivation of three areas: attention, wisdom, and values. Adapted for secular use with children and teens, they are the new ABCs of learning: attention, balance, and compassion. By learning both attention skills and a compassionate worldview, children are introduced to tools that could help them live a balanced life.

An international movement for mindful parenting and education is taking hold in cities as diverse as Lancaster, Pennsylvania; Wooster, Massachusetts; Boulder, Colorado; Oakland, California; Kalamazoo, Michigan; and Los Angeles, California, and in other countries including Singapore, Ireland, England, Germany, Mexico, and Australia. Other approaches teach productive and healthy ways of being, but lack a critical element of mindful awareness: the nonreactive, confident, and compassionate way of being alert and open to an experience as it occurs. By giving themselves enough breathing room to take in what's happening in their inner and outer worlds, children can identify both their talents and their challenges by using mindfulness techniques. The outcome is dependent on developmental capabilities (young kids are limited in what they can do by their stage of physical and emotional maturation), but those who practice mindfulness can develop a sense of balance and a calm, concentrated mind that is capable of creativity, happiness, tolerance, and compassion. With such minds children are better able to define what they want to do and achieve the goals they set for themselves. With such minds children will be ready to change the world for the better.

America now lags behind other wealthy nations in the health, education, and overall well-being of our children. Parents and citizens are alarmed, but the public outcry has been muted. Many Americans are too busy struggling to keep their own families together and their heads above water to start or even join a reform movement. Overwhelmed by the social, economic, environmental, and geopolitical problems facing our country, many are demoralized and feel that whatever they do will hardly matter—they cannot make a difference. But they can.

Mindfulness is an offer of hope. In the last century, our greatest public figures have embodied peace, compassion, and wisdom: Martin Luther King Jr., Mahatma Gandhi, Mother Teresa, the Dalai Lama, Robert Kennedy, Nelson Mandela, and, more recently, Aung San Suu Kyi. Although quite different from one another, these individuals have many characteristics in common— reflection, fearlessness, compassion, morality, perseverance, vigor, critical thinking, empathy—all qualities gained from introspection.

Perhaps the most exciting recent developments have been in the science of mindfulness. Through rigorous studies at major universities, scientists have shown how systematic and deliberate meditation practice can physically change the adult brain in ways that are beneficial and objectively quantifiable. Of course, these researchers are pointing to something many parents intuitively know—that there are psychological and ethical benefits to reflection and introspection. If you don't have a regular meditation practice yet, I encourage you to develop one. You can affect your own peace of mind.

Mindfulness Together

For millennia, poets, contemplatives, musicians, artists, and novelists have, in various ways, shapes, forms, and colors, attempted to convey the essential nature of mind. My guess is there are two things upon which they would all agree: that it cannot be captured or explained with words (like the classic Taoist teaching, "The Tao that can be spoken is not the Tao") and that the way to understand the nature of mind is through personal, direct experience.

Understanding the nature of mind does not come from the intellect alone; it's reached through a balance of intellectual comprehension and meditative experience. And since your meditation practice doesn't have to be complicated, lengthy, or formal to give you a sense of its potential, I've included short practices for you to try that are intended to be springboards for your own introspective experience. I've also included simple ways to adapt them so that you and your child can practice together. By practicing the adult exercises alone first, and then together with your child, your own meditative experience will allow your mindfulness together to flourish.

So let's get started by practicing mindful awareness and modeling it to the best of our ability, in order to pass on the incredible benefits of mindfulness to the next generation. And let's have some fun while we're doing it!

Chapter 1

An Opportunity:

Using the Science of

Mindful Awareness

May my family be filled with happiness
May my family be safe
May my family not fight
May my family be together
May my family love each other
May my family be kind
May my family care for each other
May I be full of friends
May I be safe and meet a lot of good people
May I have all the wishes I want

Sixth-grade student

In the early 2000s, I taught mindfulness at the Santa Monica Boys and Girls Club. Many other activities were going on at the same time—pool, foosball, basketball, various art projects—so at first not many kids were interested in my class, but the few who were changed my life.

A red-haired, freckled seven-year-old boy named Ezra and his impish friend Hannah were regulars in class. They were rarely apart. On Wednesday afternoons, I set up camp on the floor of the art room with cushions, rubber frogs, stopwatches, and puzzles.

Children came and went as they pleased, without being pressured to participate. Hannah and Ezra ran in and out of the group, too. Neither found it easy to focus for very long or to sit still comfortably for more than a couple minutes.

After I had been teaching for about six months, another teacher from the after-school program came to watch a class. She had been skeptical that kids could sit and concentrate in the noisy environment of the Boys and Girls Club, but the director had told her that he had noticed a change in the attitude and behavior of one nine-year-old boy, a new "calmness and nonaggressiveness" that was the "opposite of what he had once possessed," and she wanted to check it out. The director had described mindful awareness as "fun and peaceful" and the class as "fun with a purpose."

She and I were talking after class when Ezra ran into the art room. He was in a particularly whirling-dervish state that afternoon, even for him. My visitor took one look and said, "There is absolutely no way that kid can meditate. No way at all." She said this good-naturedly, but it felt as if she had thrown down the gauntlet, and I like a challenge.

Ezra and I walked over to the meditation cushions and sat facing each other. I placed a green plastic frog on the floor between us, along with a large plastic stopwatch. Ezra didn't need any instruction because we had done this many times before. I clicked the start button on the stopwatch, making sure that it was visible to him so that he could check the time on his own. He put his hand on his belly, I put my hand on mine, and we both sat quietly breathing, concentrating on the feeling of the movement of our abdomens against our hands as they rose and lowered. Neither of us said a word. My job was to simply sit and accompany him as he led the way; his was to concentrate on his breathing to the exclusion of all else as long as he was comfortable doing so. When he wanted to stop, all he had to do was click the stop button on the watch. Three, five, eight minutes later we were still sitting there, a long time for adults with the noise and distraction of the art room and an extraordinary length of time for a seven-year-old who was thought to be hyperactive. Ezra hit the stop button at eleven minutes and fifty-three seconds. I didn't realize it then, but that was the death knell for my career as a lawyer.

The visiting teacher was delighted and gave Ezra a big hug. I would like to tell you that he calmly walked out of the room, focused on his mind and body, but that's not what happened. Ezra ran out of the room, bounding with his usual energy, and the other teacher asked me a question that I have since been asked countless times: Did Ezra *really* meditate? My answer, the same answer I give to this day, was that it's hard to tell. Some children can meditate, and some can't. A child's ability to meditate varies and is related to his or her capacity to direct and maintain attention. But whether or not Ezra did meditate is not important. What matters is that he was developing more stable attention skills than those he had started with. These attention skills, in turn, would allow him to look at his own and other people's life experiences clearly, with kindness, and with compassion.

Since those first classes in the Boys and Girls Club a decade ago, I have learned much more about mindfulness, education, psychology, how the human brain changes with mental training, and how to promote a healthy attunement between adults and children. The findings from all those disciplines were involved in what happened with Ezra and me that day.

Thirty years ago, while a scientist working at the University of Massachusetts, Dr. Jon Kabat-Zinn used the practice of mindfulness to develop a secular "mindfulness-based" stress-reduction program for adults, known as MBSR. In broad terms, Dr. Kabat-Zinn taught adults to hold off, for just a short while, from reacting to or even analyzing a stressful situation and rest in the experience of what is happening in order to see it clearly. And it worked. This learned skill allowed those who practiced mindfulness-based stress reduction to better control their own reactive emotions, and therefore respond, when they were ready, in a more thoughtful, calm, reasonable way. When I started practicing mindfulness with children, my goal was to follow the precedent established by mindfulness-based stress reduction and teach self-directed, calming techniques to help them become more attentive, balanced, and aware. I hoped mindfulness would help kids see their lives clearly, set thoughtful goals, provide them with tools to achieve their goals, and become more reflective and caring adults.

Mindful awareness does not depend on reaching a peaceful mental state. Plenty of times I have sat on a cushion for an extended period of time and achieved nothing even approaching a calm, concentrated mental state. This isn't failure, but an integral part of the process of developing mindfulness. It happens to everybody. The point of mindful introspection is *to bring awareness to what happens in your mind and body (your thoughts, emotions and physical sensations, for example). Not to control your mind, but to transform it.* It is a process-oriented practice. This is the polar opposite of the school day during which children are often compelled to direct every bit of their energy to a static, rigid goal, one often measured by standardized test scores. Mindfulness is a different way of looking at learning than the approach taught in most schools, and I've seen it foster the love of learning in children.

What Is a Mindful Child?

I am often asked, What does a mindful child look like? What qualities do you look for in a mindful child? How would you recognize one? There are several scientific papers that list specific behaviors, external manifestations, and psychological processes that point to whether a person is more or less mindful than another, but my favorite description of "the mindful child" was written by two of my middle-school students in their school newspaper: "After a session of Mindful Awareness, students gradually became more positive and less tired, and their stresses began to go away." This is, in my opinion, the most powerful endorsement the program could receive.

Another question parents ask is whether they should insist that their child meditate every day. The short answer is no. I never insist that kids meditate every day, or even meditate at all.

It is relatively unusual for children to practice meditation on a regular basis on their own, but some do and tell me they find solace in the calm and ease they feel while meditating. Often these are children whose parents meditate regularly and they have company in their sitting practice, both literally and figuratively. It is wonderful when this happens, but it's not the only way to benefit from mindfulness training. Rather than insisting on a regular practice, you can model regular meditation by doing it yourself. Your children may just join in.

There are a number of potential downsides to making children sit silently for an extended period of time, such as inducing paralyzing boredom; other downsides can be potentially serious. Reflecting deeply, especially while lying down in a room with other people, is not emotionally safe for everyone. Anxiety, depression, and self-consciousness are just a few of the many legitimate reasons that meditating in public may be particularly difficult for some children. It's extremely important to remember if you're working in a classroom setting with a captive audience of students that painful emotions may bubble up during introspection. It is not uncommon for thoughts and emotions to flood a child's mind with a force and intensity that is difficult, if not impossible, for them to process on their own.

Even when there is no emotional difficulty that prevents kids from introspective practice, it doesn't make sense to force them to do it. You can insist children sit still, be quiet, and exert boundaries and control in connection with their bodies, but it is impossible to exert boundaries and control over what's going on in their minds. If children are not interested, they may sit quietly, but the likelihood that they are meditating is slim. If you are not careful, meditation can become associated with punishment or discipline, particularly with kids who are accustomed to time-outs. I see my role as one of planting seeds in the minds and homes of kids and

their families. How those seeds grow is up to them. By taking a relaxed and playful approach, children are less likely to be turned off
by mindfulness practice—they may not be interested now, but perhaps they will be at some point in their lives.

Meditation is not necessary for a child to become more mindful,
although it certainly helps. If it is safe and enjoyable for your child
to meditate, he or she will benefit from practicing meditation and
other forms of introspection in order to enhance mindfulness and
heighten self-awareness. But all forms of mindfulness enhance
mindfulness and there are a number of ways to bring mindfulness
into children's lives other than sitting meditation. Many parents integrate mindfulness into their bedtime routines, and their kids find
that resting in the physical sensation of breathing helps them fall
asleep. The most popular bedtime ritual, which you can find in
Chapter 3, is called Rockabye and entails pretending to rock a
stuffed animal to sleep with your breath.

You're More Than the
Sum of Your Parts

Through remarkable advances in modern science, researchers can
now identify the chemical and neural correlates that are responsible
for a child's thoughts, emotions, and physical sensations, and connect specific components of mindfulness training to tangible benefits. These scientific advances were achieved through the hard
work of dedicated researchers the world over, scientists who set
aside preconceived notions about meditation within the academic
community and took a risky leap of faith. Just a few years ago,
studying meditation was considered soft science, not worthy of the
best researchers; nonetheless, many of them put their careers, repu-
tations, and wallets on the line to apply the scientific method to
mindfulness practice. They designed double-blind studies that are
replicable time and time again, regardless of who performs them,
and validated meditation for people who never before would have

taken it seriously. Many of those who initially looked askance at scientists working in this field now talk about mindfulness, write about it, and even meditate themselves.

Western science has moved the field of mindfulness forward and legitimized it. But neuroscience hasn't yet been able to explain the mystery of consciousness, the uniquely human experience that we are more than the sum of our parts. In an op-ed piece in the *Los Angeles Times*, Jonah Lehrer wrote:

> According to the facts of neuroscience, your head contains 100 billion electrical cells, but not one of them is you, or knows you or cares about you. In fact, you don't even exist. You are simply an elaborate cognitive illusion, an "epiphenomenon" of the cortex. Our mystery is denied.[1]

It is in this mystery of consciousness, the place where mindfulness and science meet, where our work with children begins.

Every day, as parents, we struggle with questions for which there are no easy answers and with mysteries that we do not understand. Helping our children make healthy choices is one of our most difficult jobs and one of our most profound responsibilities. Whether we realize it or not, what we do with our kids, how we talk to them, and how we schedule their time influences their characters and points them in a certain direction. It may be creative, academic, artistic, athletic, spiritual, or any one of a number of things, but what that path is, and where it points, will affect our children for years to come—often for their whole lives. How can we help our children choose their paths with integrity? To borrow from *The Teachings of Don Juan* by Carlos Castaneda and meditation teacher Jack Kornfield's *Path with Heart*, we must be sure that their paths are connected with their hearts:

> Anything is one of a million paths. Therefore, you must always keep in mind that a path is only a path; if you feel that you should not follow it, you must not stay with it under any conditions. . . . Your decision to

keep on the path or to leave it must be free of fear or ambition. I warn you. Look at every path closely and deliberately. Then ask yourself and yourself alone one question: "Does this path have a heart?" [2]

Whatever path your child may choose for him- or herself, the insights they glean practicing mindfulness will help him or her choose a path with heart.

Four Insights of Mindfulness

Mindfulness was developed over twenty-five hundred years ago in response to a commonsense insight into the nature of everyday experience: that every aspect of life somehow fits within the framework of four basic truths. In *Breath by Breath,* meditation teacher Larry Rosenberg described the four truths as: there is suffering; there is a cause for that suffering; there is an end to it; and there is a means to that end.[3] These four insights provide a road map for teaching mindfulness to children and their families.

The First Insight—
Life Has Its Ups and Its Downs

It is easy to underestimate just how stressful modern childhood can be. Many children need to figure out themselves the rules for acceptance within their crowd. This is not easy, especially since the price of failure can be high—ostracism, bullying, friendlessness. Other children, for instance, those who have trouble performing well in school and those who feel the need to perform only at the very highest levels, often face debilitating anxiety over their real or perceived failures. In families where money is an issue, where there are medical problems, or where parents are in conflict, children may go from being stressed at school to facing a stressful home environment. No matter what you do and how hard you try, no matter how good a parent you are, your children will be confronted with problems that they cannot ignore. Mindful awareness training is designed to help children put their problems into perspective by better understanding what's going on in their inner and outer worlds.

Most problems fall under the general category of *stress,* which encompasses everything from life-threatening situations to niggling chronic worries and pressures. Stress is caused by real, perceived, or potential events that tip you out of balance and activate your body's stress response system. In his book *Why Zebras Don't Get Ulcers,* Stanford University neuroscientist Dr. Robert M. Sapolsky describes what happens when the stress response kicks into gear: Energy is mobilized and delivered to the tissues that need them, heart rate, blood pressure and breathing rate increase; long-term building and repair projects are deferred until the disaster has passed, digestion, growth, immunity, and reproductive systems are inhibited. Pain is blunted, cognition sharpened, certain aspects of memory improve and stress-induced natural painkillers, or analgesia, occur.[4] The stress response can be lifesaving in an emergency, but if activated frequently over an extended period of time—because of chronic worry or prolonged emotional challenges—it can take a serious toll on our bodies and minds. We become depleted and susceptible to illness. A prolonged stress response due to anticipated stress is often more damaging than the stressor itself, not because it makes us sick, but because it increases our risk of getting sick or decreases our ability to fight off an illness that we might already have.[5]

Stress is largely subjective. Circumstances that some people find stressful do not bother others at all. Even minor problems that many people simply shrug off can cause a significant level of stress in others. This discrepancy is largely dictated by a person's genetic predisposition and his or her life experience. We don't have any control over our genetic dispositions, but there is a whole lot we can do about how we live. And mindfulness practice has been shown to help adults manage stressful life events.

The Second Insight—
Delusion Makes Life Harder Than It Needs to Be

The pursuit of a magical solution to all of childhood's problems has created a plethora of faddish enrichment programs for kids, including diets, exercise regimens, therapies, and spiritual pursuits. At their core, most of these programs benefit kids and families, but their benefits are so often exaggerated by their proponents that parents expect unrealistic outcomes. As a result, good programs lose credibility and fade away. I've met people who talk about mindfulness practice as if it's a magic wand that will give their kids access to all types of material gain: social success, academic achievement, wealth, and even fame. I want to be clear that mindfulness is not magic. There is something magical, though, about a child seeing for the first time what's happening in, to, and around her clearly, without an emotional charge. This is true even when what she sees is unpleasant.

I learned a lesson about the connection between seeing clearly and true happiness in an unlikely location: the place where I get my car washed, which also sells greeting cards. Once, just before Mother's Day, I went inside to buy a birthday card for a friend and saw an enormous display of Mother's Day cards. I immediately turned away. Up until then I had had no idea that I felt an aversion to them. So in the time-tested tradition of mindfulness, when I recognized my aversion, I turned around, breathed deeply a few times, and took in the display of cards. I noted the range of feelings, sense impressions, and physical sensations that showed up in that moment and wasn't surprised that the cards reminded me of my mom, who had recently passed away. A wave of sadness washed over me.

Before long, though, I was looking through the cards, one after another, fascinated by the sugar-sweet rhymes and illustrations of pets and sunsets. They didn't resonate with me at all. I wondered what a Mother's Day card would look like that truly reflected all the actions that are part of the real world of a mom—changing a stinking diaper, cleaning spit-up, or holding your child in the emergency room while the doctor puts in stitches. These experiences of motherhood are far from the generic, bland images on these cards. As a mom, I have learned to tolerate sights, sounds, smells, and feelings that are unpleasant, painful, and outside of my comfort zone. I have learned that pain and discomfort can be as meaningful a part of mothering as joy. I have come to love the vibrant, electric feeling that comes from being fully present in an experience, not just the sublime moments but also the unpleasant ones. True happiness, I realized, comes from clarity, just as delusion breeds unhappiness. For example, I would have never known the depth of the joy motherhood can bring if I had shut myself off from the scarier experiences. Clearly seeing and fully experiencing the hard things in life, while difficult, can lead to a healthier psychological place. By looking hard at those cards I had tried to avoid, I came to appreciate the fullness of life experience.

We parents sometimes have trouble accepting that our kids will have problems, and that some of those problems will be serious. The first step toward helping children and teens manage stress, frustration, and disappointment is to help them take a close look at the root causes of their unhappiness. There are plenty of problems that neither parents nor their kids can fix, no matter how hard they try. But problems can be managed when children and their parents clearly see what's causing them, and recognize whether or not there's anything that can be done to change the situation. The key to managing stress and other difficult situations does not always lie in the situation itself but rather in how kids and their parents respond to it.

Seeing clearly may well be the greatest gift mindfulness has to offer. There's a lot happening all the time; mindfulness helps put experiences in their proper place, and helps you measure your response so that it's in the right proportion. Ever stub your toe on something that was left where it didn't belong? The sense impression, pain (Ouch!), springs up, immediately followed by a thought (Who left it there?) and maybe an emotion (anger, for example— What a jerk!). With a more mindful approach you notice and identify all that is happening, as it is happening, but hold off putting words to it just for a moment. Clearly seeing what is happening in, to, and around you as it is happening, without bias or reactivity, is a process that leads to peace of mind, one of the most extraordinary experiences of mindfulness practice. Helping stressed-out children find a little *peace of mind* is something I care a lot about, and it's one of the aims of mindful awareness training.

Peace of mind is not the same as zoning out or going into a trance. "Zoning out" or going into a trance is *mindlessness,* the very opposite of being mindful. Everyone's attention wanders from time to time, and it's quite wonderful for children to daydream, pretend, and weave stories in their inner worlds. A little daydreaming or zoning out is beneficial. But there are times when focus is needed and zoning out is detrimental (when taking a test, for example), and at those times mindful awareness is used to interrupt daydreaming and bring a child's attention back to the task at hand. Instead of teaching children to zone out, mindfulness teaches them to see clearly.

The Third Insight—
Happiness Is in Reach

Family life provides many examples of times when happiness emerges naturally because suffering ends. The moment a colicky baby stops crying and falls fast asleep is the end of suffering for both parent and child. When your high school senior finds out that he or she is accepted to college, the anxiety that frequently visits a family during this time drops away. It's a Sunday afternoon after a particularly rough week at work, and you settle down on the couch for a nap—and then your neighbor decides to mow the lawn. Now, that's suffering! But when he puts the lawn mower back in the shed, your suffering instantly ends. Moments of happiness that occur when suffering ceases are common in daily life. But what happens if external events don't change, or if they change for the worse?

That suffering exists and that it ends are obvious facts of life, but the idea that we can choose to be happy in the midst of suffering is less obvious. Possibly the most painful part of parenting is watching your child get hurt in a way that is utterly unfair yet not being able to do anything about it. It's a well-known truism that bad things happen to good people, and good things happen to bad people. Sometimes, there's absolutely nothing we can do. But even when we can't change a difficult situation, we can choose how to respond to it.

At times a shift in perspective is all it takes to alleviate suffering. Have events in your life ever seemed so ridiculous that you started to laugh? In that moment, your suffering had ceased. Nothing had changed in the outside world, but with a shift in perspective you could laugh about what had happened and experience an oasis of happiness, if only for a moment. How about a time when you were absolutely certain that your child was making poor choices and later learned you had been mistaken?

Sometimes parents suffer when we become overattached to one idea of what is best for our kids. We've lived longer and know from experience that a few bad decisions can make life more difficult than it needs to be. So when our children don't get good grades, or don't take leadership positions in extracurricular activities, or don't seem to be working hard enough, it makes sense to be concerned that their futures could be adversely affected. We can get so caught up in worrying about what they *are not* doing though that we forget to enjoy and appreciate what they *are* doing. There are important life skills that don't win trophies but that are, nonetheless, reliable predictors of success in later life. Maybe our children are great at making friends, helping others, or rolling with the punches, and when we can catch a glimpse of them happily caring for a pet turtle or humming a tune, our perspective shifts. In a flash, we can appreciate who they are and see their strengths clearly. With that perspective it seems foolish to worry that they aren't the quarterback of the football team, lead in the school play, or on the honor roll. Nothing has changed except our perspectives—the external events remain the same—yet, suffering has dropped away. Our children are happier than we realized, and so are we.

It is a basic and profound truth that suffering can be caused by how we view a situation, and made worse by how we respond to it. The third insight of mindfulness tells us that happiness is in reach, sometimes through something as a simple shift in perspective. The fourth insight shows us how to make that shift.

The Fourth Insight—
The Key to Happiness

When something good happens, we tend to want more. Pretty quickly we begin to focus our energy on replicating it (desire). When something bad happens, we tend to do everything we can to avoid it (aversion) and may miss aspects of the otherwise negative experience that can lead to useful life lessons. Or we tend to ignore experiences about which we are neutral (indifference) and become preoccupied with something else. Desire, aversion, and indifference are common, automatic reactions to life experience, but they may cause us trouble when we don't recognize them. Consciously or unconsciously, we often spend much of our time plotting to get what we want, trying to avoid what we don't want, and ignoring everything else.

Desire and aversion are opposites, but if we're not careful, they can have the same negative effects on our present moment. When we want more or less of something, it's easy to be so focused on a past or future moment that we miss out on some, if not all, of what's happening now. It makes perfect sense to pursue happiness and avoid unhappiness, but if we're oblivious to what we're doing, we might as well be running on automatic pilot. Reacting automatically to life experience, rather than responding thoughtfully, can have hidden costs. Many parents describe their lives as a numbing, constant sense of stress, striving, and strain that is perpetuated by their feelings of desire, aversion, and indifference. It's a fool's game and deep down they know it.

The four insights of mindfulness together encourage children and parents to see their experience clearly and respond thoughtfully with compassion. Clearly seeing isn't always easy; most of us have preconceived notions that affect how we perceive things. In *The Wise Heart,* Jack Kornfield writes, "More than anything else, the way we experience life is created by the particular states of mind with which we meet it. If you are watching a high school soccer playoff and your daughter is the nervous goalie, your consciousness will be filled with worry, sympathy, and excitement at each turn of the game. If you are a hired driver waiting to pick up someone's kid, you will see the same sights, the players and ball, in a bored, disinterested way. If you are the referee, you will perceive the sights and sounds in yet another mode. . . . Pure awareness becomes colored by our thoughts, emotions and expectations."[6]

Thoughts, emotions, and expectations are the content, not the fact, of consciousness, or what Kornfield calls, "pure awareness." Believing that our impressions, thoughts, and memories are always accurate can lead to disappointment and frustration. When having an emotional reaction, it's a good idea to pull our attention back so that we can give ourselves a little breathing room before we draw a definitive conclusion about what is or is not happening. With some perspective we can better see the big picture and respond in a way that is skillful, kind, and compassionate. This clearheaded perspective is the cornerstone of living mindfully.

There is a way of living that minimizes frustration and discontent and specifically acknowledges:

- that personal growth is both a goal and a process that evolves over time with practice

- the importance of motivation and effort

- the changing nature of all things

- that everything we say and do has consequences

- that we are connected to other people and the environment in ways that we may not know or imagine.

The fourth insight shows us how to live this way. Living mindfully is a process, not a fixed characteristic or trait. None of us are perfect, but if we take this process to heart we can lead more balanced lives. People from all over the globe and from all walks of life are working together to translate the ancient system of mental and ethical training elaborated in these four insights so that children, teens, and their families find it relevant to their modern lives. I am part of that effort. It is my hope that this book will provide you with a helpful and practical context for practicing mindful awareness, as well as basic mindful awareness practices that you and your family can incorporate into your daily routine.

Mindfulness Together: A Deep Breath to Start the Day

No matter how many books and magazine articles my husband and I read about the benefits of packing backpacks, lunches, and laying out clothing before bedtime, when our kids were young, it was rare that we had everything organized for the next day before we fell asleep. And even when we did, something usually happened the next morning that foiled our well-organized plans. Getting ready for school was like performing a circus act, and sometimes we felt like we were being shot out of a cannon.

Seth and I didn't like starting each day in a frenzy, so we instituted a morning ritual that served us well. After completing the mad rush to get ready but before leaving the house, we stopped in the hallway to take three deep breaths together. Backpacks strapped over the kids' shoulders, car keys in pockets, and briefcases in hand, we took a few breaths together to help transition into the outside world calmly. Doing this facilitated a meaningful shift in our pace and perspectives before heading out to meet the new day. I encourage you to try it if your mornings can be hectic, too.

Chapter 2

Getting Started:

Understand and Fuel

Your Motivation

To be under stress,
To have a mess,
Inside.
To sit 'n' hide.
I am happy to clean my mind.
Thank you so much for helping my stress.

Middle-school student

When my daughter, Allegra, was eight, and my son, Gabe, was five, we took them to a neighborhood Zen Center to participate in a family program. This was their first experience with meditation outside of our home. The meditation center was an old house on landscaped grounds. As our family walked through the gardens before the session, Seth and I tried to instill in the kids a sense of quiet and reverence. I told them about where we were and what we would be doing. They probably would have preferred staying at home, but they followed along respectfully. As I pointed out this plant and that flower, my daughter got something caught in her throat. She made throat-clearing noises, hacked, and then spat into the bushes.

She turned to me and said, laughing bashfully, "I think I just hawked on the holy plants!" It was hard for Allegra to take my interest seriously, but to her credit, she tried. Gabe, of course, found his sister's behavior hysterically funny, but he tried, too.

After that inauspicious beginning, we headed into the house, where parents and their children were assembling for a meditation circle. There were about fifteen people in total. I was eager to see how my kids would like it. My daughter was quite poised at that age, despite her recent assault on the "holy plants," but my son was younger and more rambunctious. I stole a glance at Gabe as the leader prepared to begin the meditation session. There he was, seated on his cushion, collecting himself, ready to go. A gong was struck, and the session began. The group leader told us we would meditate for about fifteen minutes—parents and children together. Seth caught my eye. Then he rolled his. Meditating for fifteen minutes with young children seemed overambitious. And it was.

The first thirty seconds went by, and I looked over at my son. So far, so good. He had barely fidgeted. Another minute passed, and he was still hanging in there. I was thrilled. Another minute crept by, and he had barely moved. Amazing! But after five minutes, Gabe looked at my husband, next to whom he was seated, and plaintively inquired, "How much longer do I have to pretend someone stole my brain?" Taking this as a cue, Seth led him out of the room. Together they walked in the garden (no doubt observing the "holy plants") until the meditation had ended. My sweet son did not want to sit on a cushion, didn't want to observe his thoughts, didn't enjoy the experience, but was game enough to try because I had asked him to. An open heart is the key to a mindful life. At the very least, I knew that was something he already had.

There's an old Tibetan proverb: "Mindfulness rests on the tip of motivation." Between my daughter's throat clearing and my son's frustration with having to pretend "someone stole [his] brain," I recognized it was time for me to take a look at *my* motivation for wanting *them* to learn mindfulness meditation. Was it for them, or for me, or for both? Without question, I had been motivated by universal, human desires that spring from good intentions. But when I looked closely, I had to acknowledge that part of my motivation was personal. I wanted my kids to understand what I was doing all those hours I spent sitting on a cushion meditating. I wanted them to love it, too, and to respect me for doing it. I also wanted to change them, to give them skills to help with certain aspects of their personalities that I thought could use a little bolstering. These aren't necessarily bad motivations, but they were problematic because up until that point they had not been conscious.

I learned this the hard way after our family took that historic trip to the Zen Center. Our kids didn't want to sit on a cushion and observe their thoughts, and Gabe didn't enjoy the experience. Without a doubt asking them to give it a try was appropriate, but making Gabe tough it out until the end of the session would not have been. Compulsory mindfulness is an oxymoron. Had I forced him to continue once it was clear he no longer wanted to, it would have defeated the purpose.

Mindfulness comes more naturally to some and less so to others. This is often more obvious with children, who lack the guile to hide their disinterest, than with adults. Some will like the quiet and calm of introspection; others will be indifferent to it; still others will have a hard time not bouncing off the walls. Ultimately, children will come to mindfulness in their own time and at their own pace. Now we laugh about Allegra "hawking on the holy plants" and Gabe pretending that "someone stole [his] brain." But the story is more than a family joke. It is an honest reflection of an early attempt at mindfulness from a child's point of view and an important reality check for me. From this, I learned that the first step in developing a mindfulness practice is to identify the motivation for doing so, in both the parent and the child.

Spotlight on Motivation

When I started working with kids more formally, parents sought me out to help their children with specific issues: some parents wanted their childrens' academic performance to improve; others wanted to give their kids calming skills; others hoped to instill conflict resolution skills; still others wanted to introduce a spiritual dimension. All of these goals were laudable, but they also attached a purpose to the practice, which, if left unacknowledged, could make mindfulness simply another enrichment activity to further our own (and our childrens') ends. Striving toward a sports trophy. Striving toward good grades. Even striving toward spirituality.

In a 1993 interview on PBS, Bill Moyers asked Dr. Jon Kabat-Zinn about the purpose of meditation, and he replied, "I would say that there is no purpose in meditation. As soon as you assign a purpose to meditation, you've made it just another activity to try to get someplace or reach some goal." When Moyers pointed out that people attend his stress reduction programs for a purpose, Dr. Kabat-Zinn responded, "That's true. The people in the program are all here for a purpose. They were all referred by their doctors in order to achieve some kind of improvement in their condition. But paradoxically, they are likely to make the most progress in this domain if they let go of trying to get anywhere." [1]

Undeniably, there is a goal or end result that we hope to achieve when we practice mindfulness with our children. However, emphasizing an outcome may undermine the practice itself. By taking a realistic assessment of what you hope to accomplish by teaching your kids mindfulness and why you wish to do so, you can balance these two sometimes competing objectives.

Here is an activity through which you can discover your own hopes and your child's feelings about mindfulness practice, so that you can begin your journey with a healthy, productive approach to learning.

The Five Whys is a method that I use when considering the question of motivation. This method was first developed in and used by Toyota Motor Company as a tool to evolve their design and manufacturing methodologies, and it has been refined by meditation teacher Ken McLeod to probe emotional material. The method works on the principle that the nature of a problem and its solution become clear when you ask and answer a question five times.

THE FIVE WHYS

This method is practiced in dyads, with one person asking questions and the second person answering them. The person who asks the questions listens carefully to the other person's response, and then repeats that response back in the form of another question. The person asking the questions does not formulate theories about the other person's answers, nor does he offer advice. The aim is for the person being asked the question to discover the answer him- or herself.

State a question that serves as a starting point:

Why do you want to practice mindfulness with kids?

Response:

Because I want to help ease children's suffering.

First Why

Why do you want to help ease children's suffering?

Response:

Because children are in a lot of pain right now.

Second Why

Why are children in a lot of pain right now?

Response:

Because life is just too hard.

Third Why

Why is life too hard?

Response:

Because the ethical foundation of society has crumbled.

Fourth Why

Why has the ethical foundation crumbled?

Response:

Because people are scared and looking out only for themselves.

Fifth Why

Why are people scared?

Response:

Because they don't see the big picture and that everything is connected.

The Five Whys is a fun activity to play with kids, too. With young children I use this game to help them learn how to listen carefully, and practice doing it. I don't use it to probe emotional material with little kids. Instead, I ask very simple questions like "Why do you like animals?" or "Why do you like chocolate?" The answers tend to get silly fairly quickly, but that's okay, even when answers are silly children must listen carefully to formulate an appropriate why question in response.

Well-meaning and enthusiastic adults can become frustrated when I ask them to consider their motivation before they learn the mindfulness games and activities I use with kids. They're eager to get started and want to skip over this inquiry into their own process. But understanding motivation is, in fact, the first step in mindfulness training. Asking and answering the Five Whys is a good place to begin.

It's as important to ask kids about their motivation as it is to ask adults. My students are often a captive audience—brought in by parents, sent by classroom teachers, referred by therapists—so I never take it personally if one of them tells me he or she was at first skeptical or reluctant to see me. One of many refreshing things about working with this age group is that kids tend not to shy away from tough questions like: Why are you here? Did your parents make you take this course? Or the follow-ups: Even if your parents forced you to sign up for this class, is there something positive you can take away from it? Are there any life or social skills that you'd like to learn or build upon? When I ask kids about their motivation, I encourage them to hold off on analyzing the question, but instead to check in with the reservoir of knowledge stored in their bodies to see how the question *makes them feel.* Ever have a funny feeling that you were absolutely sure was a reliable indicator of something, even though you had no idea of what? That's an example of how body-based awareness can bypass the thinking mind. The kinks in your neck, the butterflies in your stomach, and the throbs in your forehead store volumes of information. With practice, students recognize important signals that come from their bodies and give them weight equal to those that come from their minds.

A classical image used to evoke an inept approach to learning mindfulness is that of three defective pots. There are three ways for a pot to be defective: when it is upside down, when it has a hole in it, or when it contains poison. An upside-down pot is always empty, no matter how much water you pour over it, like a distracted child who retains bits and pieces of mindfulness training but never catches the whole picture. A child who meditates but doesn't integrate mindfulness into daily life is like a pot with a hole that leaks water as quickly as it's poured in. A child afflicted by an unfriendly or wrongheaded motivation is like a pot containing poison. The poison taints the water within and is, by far, the most serious defect.[2] By talking through our motivations, we can work with children to make them like an upright, strong pot—open to new experience and ready to learn.

Kids often turn the question of motivation around to ask me why I teach mindfulness. It's only fair that I'm as candid as I ask them to be. So I tell them that, at first, I was looking for tools to help me concentrate and manage stress, but soon I learned there's a lot more to mindfulness than that. The more I practiced, the more balanced my life became and the happier I felt. What's more my family, and pretty much everyone around me, seemed happier when I practiced, too. But these benefits were not always easy to come by. Balance came only when I was willing to take a clear-eyed look at what was going on in my life, recognize it, and then make a change if necessary. Changing was (and often still is) the hard part, but it wouldn't have been mindfulness if I hadn't worked to integrate what I learned from practice into my life.

Walking the Dogs:
Intention, Ardency, and Perseverance

Even when our motivation is sincere, there are times when we don't feel like meditating. That feeling is only natural, but through a combination of intention, ardency, and perseverance, we practice anyway. Setting the intention to do something is the first step in any form of discipline; ardency is the mental wherewithal to follow through; and perseverance is actually doing so. Intention, ardency, and perseverance allow us to move beyond resistance and attend to the task at hand.

This triad shows up when I walk our dogs, Rosie and Lucy. Although inseparable, they couldn't be more different from each other: Rosie is an enthusiast and loves to hike, but Lucy is not so sure. When it comes to hiking, my mind is like my dogs. There are times I feel like Rosie and want to hike, and then there are times when, like Lucy, hiking is the last thing I want to do. When I feel like Lucy, I remember the classical image of "crushing the mind with itself" and picture the cartoon character Popeye with a thought bubble over his head. In my imagination, Popeye's thought bubble contains an enormous barbell just waiting to drop down and crush his mind if it wanders from the task at hand. This image of Popeye with his barbell is quite useful for adults, but somewhat heavy-handed for children. Setting your mind to do something that isn't appealing, digging your heels in, and doing it anyway is an extremely useful mental muscle that is developed by practicing mindfulness. On those days when pretty much anything, even laundry or cleaning out my desk drawers, is more appealing than hiking, I grit my teeth, pull on my hiking shoes, and try to get myself out on the trail anyway. I'm not always successful, but it helps if I remind myself that the very activities I dread sometimes make me happier, healthier, and more balanced.

The discipline of getting out of the house and on the hiking trail is just the first step. To go the distance, I sometimes need to renew my intention many times. There are always valid reasons to cut the hike short and head home: it looks like it's going to rain; I'm tired; I'm hungry; I need to call my sister. But in the face of these excuses, I persevere because I know that talking myself out of being distracted and back into hiking is part of the process. It's the same with practicing meditation. Spotting distractions and recovering from them is as much a part of meditation as resting in a calm and peaceful mental state. Meditation and distraction coexist. The object is not to rid your environment of distractions but to recognize them and resist engaging. For example, when practicing mindfulness of breathing, the instant you become aware that you're distracted and redirect your attention back to your breath is, by definition, an act and an experience of mindful awareness. Kids know this, too. Recently, I asked a middle school class to break into small groups to discuss how they incorporate mindfulness into their daily routines. When the class reconvened, one group reported that they spent most of the discussion period off topic, talking about their upcoming semiformal. When the bell signaled that time was up, the group realized they had gotten sidetracked and had nothing to report to the large group. They proudly announced that noticing they were distracted and hadn't discussed the assignment was an example of how they integrated mindful awareness into daily life.

We all have trouble staying on task sometimes. Walking the dogs every day, keeping a conversation on topic, and meditating every day—like all other disciplined activities—require ardency and perseverance. When practicing mindfulness, the application of the two is rarely a linear process, but rather a gentle progression that resembles the flight pattern of a moth toward a flame. The moth is drawn to the light, but as it gets closer to the flame, it also gets hotter. If the moth flies in too close, it risks getting burned. So when it gets too hot for the moth to bear, it flies away from the flame, circles around, and tries again. Over and over the moth swoops toward the flame and then backs off, getting closer and closer with each attempt as the fire dies down and the flame fades. Nowhere is this more true than when bringing mindful awareness to difficult emotions. The practice of drawing closer to an emotion time and time again, only to the extent at which you are able to do so comfortably, allows adults and teens an opportunity to explore the edges of their feelings, little by little, and develop a capacity to hold the emotion in attention, which ultimately can allow them to better understand it. This practice requires a level of attentional and emotional maturation that is out of reach for young children.

Commonsense Advice

I'd like to share three pieces of commonsense advice for helping your kids stay focused on the mindfulness practices described in the chapters to come:

> Keep it simple.
> Keep it fun.
> Keep your sense of humor.

Keep It Simple

When I first started teaching mindfulness to kids, I needed a suitcase to carry all my paraphernalia with me to class. Before leaving the house, I filled a duffel bag with drums of different shapes and sizes, pinwheels, decks of cards, stopwatches, rubber ducks and frogs, a CD player, stuffed animals, notebooks, pencils, crayons and pastels, tambourines, rain sticks, Tibetan singing bowls, tuning forks, cushions, blankets, stickers, charts, puzzles, picture books, snacks, juice boxes. . . . You would have thought I was going to a swap meet. There are prop comedians who lug less gear onstage than I brought to those classes. But I wanted all of this stuff to hold children's interest as we played games intended to simplify their lives. At the time, I didn't see the irony.

After my first year of teaching, I gave up the suitcase and got everything into a backpack. I no longer needed to hire a roadie, but it was still a lot of stuff. Today, I walk into class with my dulcimer or my guitar, a few small, smooth stones in my pocket, and a canvas bag that contains a tone bar, a card called a mind meter, flip charts, and a tambourine. Sometimes I bring a drum, too, or supplies for the game we're playing that day. I view this transition from a suitcase to a backpack to a small canvas bag as a metaphor for my development as a teacher. Over the years I have learned to trust more in the practice of mindfulness itself and less in what accompanies it.

The same held true with the evolution of the mindfulness games I play with kids; ultimately, I fine-tuned them by adapting absolutely every word and activity so they would be fun and accessible for a four-year-old. After I had been teaching students ages seven and older for several years, I got a call from Dr. Sue Smalley, a professor at UCLA who was interested in studying the effect of mindfulness on kids. I agreed to meet with her and subsequently learned that she was a geneticist who studied ADHD. She had recently had a health crisis, discovered meditation, and, like so many of us, figured it had been so beneficial to her that it surely could be important to kids as well.

She asked me over coffee if I thought pre-K students could be taught mindfulness. It was hard for me to imagine that kids so young would be receptive to mindfulness practice, but I agreed to give it a try. And it worked, but it required me to change my program a bit. Like paring down my traveling curiosity shop to only as much as I could carry, simplifying my practices so they would be accessible to preschoolers was a powerful practice for me. As French philosopher Blaise Pascal wrote in the seventeenth century, "I'm sorry this letter is so long. I didn't have time to write a shorter one." It takes a long time and a lot of trial and error to distill concepts to their bare minimum, but it is well worth the effort. I was surprised when the simple exercises and language developed for little kids resonated better with older children and teens than the more complicated activities I had typically used with them. And even more surprising, a number of parents and professionals told me they gained a better understanding of mindfulness through the matter-of-fact practices intended for very young children than they had after years of taking classes and reading mindfulness books. No one says it better than Henry David Thoreau: "Simplify, simplify, simplify."

Keep It Fun

It's nearly impossible to concentrate when you're hungry or tired, and certainly it's not fun. I cannot tell you how many times kids have come to mindfulness class hungry, tired, or both.

One challenging experience was teaching an after-school class to middle-school students between four to five in the afternoon. One of the girls who came regularly was miserable during the first class. Kids are often uncomfortable for one reason or another, but she couldn't sit still for more than a minute or two. I asked what was wrong, and she told me she was hungry. It made a lot of sense that she couldn't concentrate and also that her father didn't have time to get her a snack before class. I promised that I'd bring snacks next time. The following week I brought healthy snacks to class, and everyone was appreciative. It turned out that the girl who had had a hard time concentrating was not the only one who had been hungry during the previous class. We ate granola bars after introspection, chomped on carrot sticks as we sat in a circle talking about mindfulness, and drank from juice boxes before sending friendly wishes.

The kids were having fun, and I was pleased, until the girl's father came to pick her up. He surveyed the room, saw the leftovers, and asked me to step out on the porch to speak with him. He kindly but firmly thanked me for the class before he told me that his daughter was not to be given food again before, after, or during class. I asked why, thinking the girl might have a medical condition

I wasn't aware of. The girl was heavy, but nothing about her struck me as outside the range of normal. Because, her father told me, the reason he had enrolled his daughter in this class was to ensure she was busy in the afternoon and wouldn't be able to eat.

It's easy to miss the connection between food and attention. It's not uncommon in workshops for parents to voice concerns about their children's attention problems and getting them to settle down and do homework right after school. When I ask parents if they've tried giving children a snack before starting the homework routine, they are often surprised. Once it's pointed out, most parents recognize that giving kids a healthy snack before (and sometimes during) homework helps them concentrate. In addition to the connection between eating and concentration, researchers have found a stunning connection between eating together as a family on a regular basis and decreased substance abuse among kids and teens.[3]

A similar connection exists between sleep and attention. It's extremely hard to concentrate when you're sleepy, and there is a well-established connection between insufficient amounts of sleep and a decline in children's school performance. Lack of sleep not only adversely affects a child's cognitive abilities; it has also been linked to health issues.

The same holds true when children are overscheduled. Sometimes an overzealous commitment to education can take the fun out of learning. Just look at the increasingly competitive application process to get into a "good" school. In some parts of the country, the level of competition once reserved for college admissions has extended to secondary schools, elementary schools, and even preschools. In these areas, it is common for parents of toddlers to experience stress over the prospect of finding a suitable preschool. While toddlers may not understand the cause of the stress, they experience it vicariously through their well-meaning parents.

The pressure doesn't let up once a child is accepted; from there, the child's time is devoted to more achievement, through extracurricular activities and sometimes excessive tutoring—which can have hidden costs, including undermining a child's confidence and making it hard for schools to assess the effectiveness and pace of their curricula. I have sympathy for parents who want only the best for their children—I count myself as one of them—and this "irrational commitment" of a parent to a child, a term coined by British psychologist and parenting expert Penelope Leach in 1997, is a critical building block of healthy parent-and-child relationships. But the knee-jerk need to "keep up with the Joneses" in matters of education and achievement can backfire.

Children aren't the only ones who are overscheduled and overprogrammed. When asked what would ease their workaday burden, parents often say more time, explaining that there just aren't enough hours in the day to do what needs to be done. But fortunately, parents have more time than they feel they have. Parents take on many elective activities that they think will be good for their children without fully considering their hidden costs. As if by habit, parents become overscheduled, overprogrammed, and overcommitted, and their kids do, too. Both parents and children are frequently so busy they forget that all of the *doing* can take away from just *being* together.

When was the last time your child spent an afternoon just noodling around in the backyard or living room, playing make-believe, building with blocks, or climbing trees, with only the aid of his or her imagination? Many parents worry about the potential negative effect of an ever-increasing decrease in unscheduled, unstructured playtime on children. Educators voice similar concerns. Dr. Paul Cummins, executive director of the New Visions Foundation and founder of the Crossroads and New Roads schools in California, told me, "My wife's a piano teacher, and we know that if you don't start a child at a certain age there's a kind of flexibility of the fingers that you can't recapture if you try to start at twenty, thirty, forty, fifty years old. Something is lost. It's just an article of faith, but I believe that if you rob children of their childhood, you've robbed them of something that's fundamentally crucial, and, if not irretrievable, it makes it much harder to retrieve it." Cummins continued, "How many people do we know who are *imagination-less*. They don't know it, but their lives are diminished."[4]

You can barely turn on the TV or pick up a newspaper without seeing an article about ADHD, but that morning Cummins and I put aside worries about how well kids can pay attention and wondered how an *imagination deficit disorder*, or IDD, would affect young people as they move into adulthood. Cummins commented, "We so overprogram children that reflection is virtually impossible. We've got third graders doing homework; it's absurd. The homework that children should be doing is playing; when we try to program play out of childhood, I think we do developmental harm."

University of British Columbia researcher Dr. Adele Diamond has expressed concern that lack of unstructured playtime could adversely affect the development of young children's planning and organizational skills. Diamond's study followed 147 preschool-age children who were taught a curriculum, Tools for the Mind, that includes dramatic play as part of the regular school day. The preschoolers showed notable improvement in executive function, or planning and organization skills. In a study published in *Science* magazine, Diamond wrote, "Although play is often thought frivolous, it may be essential [to the development of executive function]."

From the point of view of mindfulness there is an additional downside to being run-down, overscheduled, tired, or hungry: a loss in perspective. When we don't take care of ourselves, our ability to see events in our lives clearly and objectively decreases. Children need to be well rested and well fed to be successful learners. When we cut corners on family meals and exhaust our children in pursuit of achievement, it becomes much more difficult, if not impossible for them to develop the nonreactive, clear mind-set necessary to achieve their goals. And no less important, they stop having fun.

Keep Your Sense of Humor

I give my adult students (usually parents, educators, and health care professionals interested in practicing mindfulness with kids) three additional pieces of practical advice for teaching mindfulness to kids: First, make your peace with the fact that, when you ask kids to be mindful, they'll bust you when you are not mindful yourself. And, of course, none of us is mindful all the time. Second, keep it real by teaching only what you have directly experienced. And third, the path you've chosen will be far easier if you keep your sense of humor. To quote hippie sage Wavy Gravy, "If you don't have a sense of humor, it just isn't funny anymore."

The mindfulness practices adapted in this book require far more training and understanding than the dictionary definition of mindfulness—"to take heed"—suggests. Many who have devoted their lifetimes to mastering these practices believe they have just scratched the surface. But you don't need to wait until you've completed years of study before practicing mindfulness with your children, provided you follow one very important rule of thumb: *Teach only what you know from direct experience.* I cannot emphasize this single point enough. If you read about an interesting aspect of meditation, and have not experienced it yourself, don't teach it. Kids have a nose for what's authentic and what's not.

One of the classroom teachers I worked with asked me this question: "I'm not a piano teacher, but I can play 'Baa Baa Black Sheep' on the piano, and I teach my preschoolers to play 'Baa Baa Black Sheep' on the piano. Can I teach mindfulness even though I've had only a couple of months of training?" Absolutely. She *absolutely could* teach what she'd learned to her preschool students, but I cautioned her to teach only the mindfulness equivalent of "Baa Baa Black Sheep." At that point she had a solid understanding of the calming qualities of breath awareness and how those qualities could help young kids, so she integrated these practices into the classroom and I was delighted to learn that her students were enthusiastic participants. Other teachers have gotten into trouble, however, by trying to teach something they hadn't yet experienced themselves. This is dangerous territory and can raise ethical issues. That said, you can share the joy of mindfulness with kids, even while you're still learning, by "trying on" a practice from the outside in, as you continue to work on embodying it from the inside out. "Trying on a practice" means getting a feel for it by going through its steps and familiarizing yourself with what it entails, even though you don't yet completely understand the process or the theory behind it. As your practice evolves, you'll be able to try new things.

Practical Applications

Here are a few guidelines to help you get started:

- Find a support system to accompany you along this path; it's important to find an established mindfulness teacher and connect with others who already meditate regularly and have done so for a while.

- People mature at different rates and the more sophisticated concepts in mindfulness are out of reach for many children and teens. It doesn't mean that they won't ever be able to grasp these concepts, only that they aren't ready to grasp them yet. Don't push them beyond their comfort level.

- When meditating with kids, remember that you don't know everything about their inner and outer lives, even if they are your own children. Tread carefully when children discuss painful emotional issues, and don't be afraid to seek help from a professional if a child says something that troubles you or if he or she is in a great deal of emotional pain.

- Don't insist that a child meditate, or discuss painful emotions, if he or she doesn't want to.

- Put aside any judgment or analysis while practicing mindfulness, and commit yourself to the experience. Thoughts about what you like, what you don't like, how great the kids are doing, how you wish you had had this opportunity when you were a child, how silly the practices may be, how profound . . . this type of analysis is natural. But by practicing, you will develop a different relationship with thinking. You'll learn that there will be plenty of time for reflection and analysis after you meditate.

- See if you can become comfortable with "not knowing" or at least "not knowing yet." If you have questions about meditation while meditating, be sure to follow up on them, but not until afterward. An understanding will emerge naturally through the practice.

- Set boundaries for kids in a way that is consistent with the principles of mindful awareness. This can be challenging, but here are some basic tricks of the trade for setting mindful boundaries, some of which are also tried-and-true classroom management tools that work just as well at home:

  - Use every opportunity to communicate with your child nonverbally. For example, if a child is speaking out of turn, rather than asking him or her to stop, you might make eye contact, smile, and put your finger to your lips, or your hand to your ear, or point in the direction of where the child should focus his or her attention.

  - The "silence" or "hands-up" signal is an effective classroom management tool that you can bring home. The idea is that when you raise your hand, everyone who can see you does the same. When your hands are up, it means there should be no talking and that eyes and ears should be on you. A variation on the silent signal is to use a verbal cue asking for a nonverbal gesture in response. If your kids are engaged in an activity and not likely to see you raise your hand, just say, "If you hear my voice, raise your hand." Again, raising hands means that voices should be quiet and eyes and ears should be on you.

- Be aware of how you're moving and see if you can move more slowly than your usual pace. It's fun to move in slow motion and it helps kids become more deliberate when they move, and more aware of where their bodies are in relation to other people and things. It also helps children maintain a more mindful mental state as they shift their attention from one activity to another.

- When practicing mindfulness together, your child's and your focus should be on the same activity. If you're keeping your child company while she practices, it can be confusing to her if you focus on one thing while she focuses on another. By directing your attention to the object of the mindful awareness practice (the drum, your breath, a stuffed animal on your belly), you model where your child's attention should be focused during the practice.

- Be as consistent as possible, and integrate mindful awareness into your daily activities. None of us is perfect (just ask my family), but the more you integrate mindfulness, the more your kids will do so and the more mindfulness will become second nature.

- Give yourself a break. Cultivate patience, and remember there's a learning curve. Mindfulness comes with practice.

- Be spontaneous and creative when practicing with your child. If you think of a way to integrate mindfulness into something you're already doing together, give it a try. There's an infinite number of mindfulness activities waiting to be discovered as you wash dishes, fold clothes, do homework, play games, answer the telephone, and work on the computer.

If you're looking for advice for integrating mindfulness into your family life in a meaningful way, the best I can give you is to establish a regular meditation practice, hopefully with friends or family, and embrace from it what resonates with you. Use your own meditation experience as your compass when working with kids. I've seen people try to teach the way someone else—perhaps their own meditation teacher or a famous one—teaches. That tends not to work very well. Some of us are more comfortable with analytical practices, others with compassion. Some of us are better with music, some with art, some with movement. Practice what's true for you. But, most important, practice. And if it doesn't come easily at first, don't worry. Just keep practicing.

Your Mindfulness Practice:
Finding Others to Accompany You

Meditating in a group of like-minded friends can support our meditation practice and help us to integrate mindfulness into daily life. Groups provide support and encouragement and can enhance the participants' meditation experiences because everyone in the group benefits from one another's efforts. The aim of a meditation group is to support the personal discovery of each participant, not to give advice or solve one another's problems. The group acts as a mirror for each member; I think the Velvet Underground song by Lou Reed sums it up nicely: "I'll be your mirror, reflect who you are in case you don't know."

The eye cannot see its own pupil is a teaching that captures a fundamental conundrum in the study of the nature of mind. Meditation is the study of our own minds, and as we set out on this study, we must overcome the limitation that the mind cannot see itself. But even though we can't directly see our faces, we have seen them reflected in the mirror, and we know how they look. The role of those who accompany others in the practice of mindfulness is to act as a mirror and reflect someone's words and actions just as a mirror reflects the image of a someone's face. Skillfully reflecting another's meditative experience is an art, a deeply moving and supportive experience for all those involved, and doing so requires training and guidance as projections and perceptions often can get in the way. We make every effort to support one another (and ourselves) in the process of turning, returning, and turning again into our experiences to discover what's hidden inside of us. A sitting group works as a mirror in another important way: by watching our own minds as we participate in the group, we act as a mirror for ourselves.

You don't need a lot of people to create a support system for your meditation practice. One other person is enough. Here are some guidelines:

- When we accompany one another in meditation practice, we:

  - Observe our own minds and act as a mirror *for ourselves* by noticing how we react to other people's experience and how we react to our own.

  - Listen with kindness and compassion as other people describe their meditation experiences.

  - Act as a mirror *for others* by reflecting back their descriptions of their experiences without bias and without tainting the reflection with our own projections.

- When listening, speaking, and watching our own minds, it's helpful to remember that:

  - When we become aware of negative qualities in ourselves, and reactions that we have to other people's experiences that we're not proud of, it's important to be as kind, understanding, and empathic toward ourselves as we are to others.

  - Before asking another participant questions about his or her experience, first check your motivation. Sometimes questions that we ask other people are, in fact, cloaked questions about ourselves that spring from a desire to explore our personal experience. Sometimes we're aware of this, and sometimes we're not. Make sure that whatever questions you ask are fundamentally about other participants and are sincerely motivated by an interest in helping them in their process of personal discovery.

  - At some point in the mirroring process, it is likely that something or someone will trigger an uncomfortable feeling or reaction in you. When this happens, don't shy away from it. Instead, observe your discomfort just as you observe your meditation experiences with curiosity, kindness, and compassion.

- When accompanying others in their meditation practice, it is helpful to remember that:
    - Sympathizing with other people by talking about how their experiences resonate with you tends not to be as helpful as asking questions that point them back toward their own direct experience.
    - Guessing about what might be going on in someone else's meditation practice or drawing comparisons with your own experiences also tends not to be as helpful as asking them questions.

Mindfulness Together

Like many parents I have lived many different lives. I've lived the life of a corporate executive, of a mom, of a daughter, of a sister, of a wife, of a small-business owner, of a friend, of a volunteer, of a sick person, of someone on the way up, and of someone on the way down. In each of these lives I've had colleagues, friends, and family members with whom I've had virtually the same conversation. It goes something like this:

From a very young age, the world we live in encourages us to strive to be someone or something special. It's a world that sets people apart from one another and values achievement, glorifying results at the expense of the process. But as we mature, the pursuit of being someone or doing something special begins to seem hollow. We discover that no matter how lucky we are, even if we've achieved our wildest dreams or come pretty close, we can feel as if there's something missing. With each accomplishment, the bar is set higher. We'd like nothing more than to jump off of this merry-go-round and stop chasing an elusive gold ring, but we don't see an alternative. Is this because there isn't an alternative, or is it only a failure of our imaginations? Many would be willing to renounce the material world if they truly believed that they would be happier with less. But would walking away from accomplishment be like throwing the baby out with the bathwater? Is there a way to embrace this paradox, and better understand it, in order to celebrate the life that we already have?

You may have had similar conversations with friends and colleagues. When looking for others to join your sitting group, or simply to talk with about meditation, I encourage you to connect or reconnect with those people with whom you've questioned life and sought answers. They will be your mirrors through this journey, and you will be theirs.

Chapter 3

As Simple as Breathing:

Get Started with

Relaxation and Calming

Be full of love
Be happy and safe
Have peace
No troubles

Second-grade student

At seven a.m. on a brisk winter day in Los Angeles, I was in an elementary schoolroom sitting on a chair designed for a six-year-old. There was a translator on one side of me and a security guard on the other, and I was teaching a group of mostly Latina moms simple breath awareness techniques to help them feel better, both physically and mentally, in the midst of the enormous pressures they shouldered each day. These moms were single, victims of domestic violence and spousal abuse. My job was to teach them self-directed mindfulness techniques that they would in turn teach their children—if not through direct instruction, then through example, which is by far the most powerful teaching method that we possess as parents.

These women did not get out of bed for this early morning meeting because they had a passionate interest in mindfulness. Few, if any, of them had heard about mindfulness before reading the flyer from the shelter, and after reading about it many did not have a favorable impression. Most were devout Catholics, and some thought mindfulness was a mystical religion. Others thought it was some New Age California thing. They were skeptical but nonetheless got to the classroom very early in order to lie on a cold floor and give mindfulness a try, because they would do pretty much anything within their power to help their kids have a chance at a better life. At the end of class, one after another, they spoke about what a relief it was to take the time for themselves to calm and quiet their minds and bodies.

At the time I was a relative newbie teaching mindfulness to kids and families, and I would sometimes look around the room and wonder, How can I be so certain that these simple breathing techniques, the same ones that had helped me get through a particularly traumatic time in my own life, would be of help to anyone else? It was one thing to work with privileged kids whose parents were able to provide an abundance of enrichment activities for them. After all, teaching kids mindfulness isn't going to hurt anyone, and at least it helps them see something in a new way, however briefly.

I didn't feel the same way teaching in the domestic violence center. In underserved areas, time and energy are resources as scarce as money, and for my own peace of mind I had to be 100 percent certain that what I was teaching would help these families, and not just help a little. It had to be such a big help that it justified not only asking these kids and moms to get out of bed early in the morning, but, more important, getting their hopes up.

Almost a decade later, I've seen the benefits of mindfulness manifest in many different cultures, every age group, and across continents. I don't have those doubts anymore.

Finding What's Already Here

The natural clarity of everyone's minds can be hidden by the restless mental chatter of daily experience. Imagine you're looking at the surface of a pond. When the water is still, you can see through it to the sand and stones on the bottom. But on a windy day, when there are waves and ripples on the surface of the water, you can't see what's underneath. Mental restlessness can be like wind on the surface of a pond, making ripples and waves that hide the still, clear mind below. Introspection calms the waves so that we can once again see through the still water to the bottom of the pond. The process of introspection settles restless thoughts and emotions, allowing us to discover the stillness and mental clarity that is already here. It's not easy to explain this concept to children with words alone, but you can get the point across with the aid of a cylinder of water and some baking soda.

CLEAR MIND GAME

Take a clear glass cylinder full of water, put it on a table, and ask your children to look through and see what's on the other side. They'll probably see you or whatever's sitting on the tabletop. Pour a cupful of baking soda in the water and shake the cylinder. What does it look like now? Can they still see through to the other side? Probably not: the baking soda clouds the water and obscures their vision. Just like baking soda in water, thoughts and emotions can create havoc in our heads and cloud our otherwise clear minds. After a minute or two, take another look at the water. What happens when you leave it alone? Sure enough, the more the water rests, the more the baking soda settles, and the clearer the water becomes. Soon, all the baking soda will settle to the bottom of the cylinder and your children will be able to see through the glass again. The same holds true with our minds. The longer we rest in the steady rhythm of our breathing, the more our thoughts and emotions settle down and the clearer our minds become.

In his book *Zen Mind, Beginner's Mind*,[1] Suzuki Roshi describes a clear mind as "beginner's mind," a mind like a child's. Beginner's mind reflects a mental state that is open and receptive, one of nonreactive, nonconceptual awareness. It's not empty, but it's a lens through which we experience life directly and clearheadedly. I explain this way of seeing and experiencing life by comparing two different perspectives on a rainbow. Someone who knows that a rainbow exists but has never seen one him- or herself has a conceptual perspective that is quite different from that of someone who has actually seen and experienced the magic of a rainbow in the afternoon sky.

A beginner's mind is open and receptive to new ideas, not closed down by adhering rigidly to what he or she believes to be true. Putting preconceived concepts and ideas aside to look at something with fresh eyes is one of the most difficult qualities to cultivate in mindfulness practice, and it isn't easy to describe. But I stumbled upon a way to do so when I least expected it. Making breakfast one morning when my kids were younger, I opened up a cylindrical box of Quaker Oats cereal and was taken by surprise. Instead of finding oatmeal, I found a treasure trove of brightly colored and shiny glass jewels that my daughter had hidden away. Somehow her Quaker Oats treasure chest had made its way back into the kitchen cupboard. When I saw what was inside, my expectations were jettisoned, and I experienced a moment of nonconceptual knowing—a flash of awareness—in that shattering of the bustle of my morning routine. "Aha," I said to myself. This is a way to begin a discussion with kids about beginner's mind. So I put the oatmeal box in my backpack and headed out to teach. Since then I've used a Quaker Oats box many, many times as a visual aid in a mindfulness game I call What's Inside the Box.

WHAT'S INSIDE THE BOX

Take an empty box of Quaker Oats or another cereal and put something fun inside. For example, a set of colorful jacks, a toy car, or Legos. Place it in the middle of the circle of children, or on a table with your own children, and ask them to guess what, besides cereal, could possibly be inside the tall cylindrical box. I've heard guesses that ranged from "oatmeal" to "lizards." After everyone has had a turn guessing, ask the kids questions about what it feels like not to know what's in the box. Do they want to know? Have there been times in their lives when something was going on and they didn't know what it was? What was that like? How does it feel to be really curious and eager to discover? Sit with the kids and pay attention to what it feels like not to know something. Ask them how their bodies feel when they don't know what is going to happen next. Is it comfortable? Is it uncomfortable? Does anyone feel excited? Ask them if it feels like they have butterflies in their stomachs. See if you and the kids can feel the energy and thrill of not knowing fill the room. If you can, just sit there and breathe, taking it all in. Now they can look inside the box!

Beginner's mind is the most natural thing in the world, but many of us have had it conditioned out of us long before adulthood. It is a child's default mind-set, but sometimes we inadvertently condition it out of them, too. When working with kids, teenagers especially, I'm reminded of a refrain from the song "Anyone Can Whistle," by Stephen Sondheim: "What's hard is simple. What's natural comes hard." Even with the best intentions, we don't always make life simple for kids.

Many of the children I teach are extremely accomplished. They get good grades, make the varsity team, solo at the concert, perform amazing feats of community service, score well on their standardized tests: you name it, they nail it. Worldly success comes relatively easily to these kids. No wonder: many of them have watched their moms and dads model achievement since they were little. Here's the good news: by modeling hard work, we've helped make difficult things, like working hard, come naturally to our kids. The flip side is that, in doing so, we sometimes make natural things—like finding the way back to a childlike, open and curious "beginner's mind"—very, very hard.

Friendliness

One way for parents and kids to find their way back to the clarity of beginner's mind is by living in a way that promotes caring, kindness, joy, equanimity, patience, generosity, humility, happiness for the good fortune of others, compassion, and service. I tell my students a story about a child who lives that way that's modeled on a classical mindfulness story.[2]

THE KIND AND GENTLE PRINCESS

Once I heard about a kind princess who lived in a magical kingdom. When she was a little girl, all the royal families in the empire sent their children to boarding schools. When the time came for the princess to go to school, she packed up her backpack, said good-bye to her parents, and headed off along a winding dirt road to the Wisdom Academy. The Wisdom Academy was a special school because wise teachers from all over the realm came there to speak. When they lectured, the scholars sat on a bejeweled throne that floated high above the courtyard and their students sat below on a lawn of the most brilliant green grass you've ever seen. The academy was famous for these lectures, and people traveled from neighboring villages and cities just to hear the golden words of the scholars.

The kind and gentle princess was excited when she reached her new school. But soon she realized she didn't fit in with the crowd. She didn't do what the other kids did, and she didn't say what the other kids said. Her friends and her teachers thought that all the kind princess did was daydream. Her professors never saw her study, and she seemed to sleep all the time; they didn't know what to make of her. So they decided to test her knowledge. The professors asked their daydreaming student to give a lecture in the courtyard, hoping that she would study so as not to embarrass herself in front of her friends and neighbors. The kind princess agreed, but still she didn't study. The day of her lecture drew near, and her professors were very, very worried.

When it was her turn to speak, the kind and gentle princess climbed up onto the throne, which was reserved for the wisest of people, and began to speak. As the kind princess spoke, a crowd of her friends and people from the neighborhood gathered in the courtyard of the academy. High up on the floating throne, the daydreaming princess told everyone about the promise she had made to herself to help everyone she met be happy. Her voice carried over the neighborhood, and soon the courtyard was filled with townspeople who had been drawn to the school grounds by what the princess was saying.

The rapt crowd heard her say that she wanted to fill people's homes with sweet music. They heard her say she wished that the sky would rain flowers in their backyards. She wanted to become a bodyguard to keep her friends and family safe from harm. She wanted to be a boat, a raft, or a bridge to help her friends cross over stormy rivers; a soft bed where people could rest when they were tired; and a flashlight for those afraid of the dark. The kind princess wanted to become a doctor to heal the sick, and a magic lamp that could make other people's wishes come true. These are just some of the friendly wishes the kind daydreamer spoke to those who heard her that day.

There is more to this story, which I will share later in Chapter 9. Right now, typing away in my bedroom, with Seth at his computer downstairs, Gabe practicing his guitar, and Allegra fighting a head cold while lying on my bed nearby, I'd like to send friendly wishes to you.

May you always keep your sense of humor.

May you have lots of fun practicing mindfulness with kids.

May you love the process of discovery that defines this work and be comfortable not knowing all the answers.

May you remember that helping children become more aware of themselves, and of others, and of the planet is serious work, indeed.

As is loving, singing, dancing, laughing, playing, and having fun.

Friendly wishes like those the kind princess and I just sent might seem a little corny, or silky, but they are a key component of mindfulness practice for kids, one that instills thoughtfulness and compassion. And it might sound familiar to you if you've already encountered the classical practice of loving-kindness.

Sending Friendly Wishes

My favorite classical practices cultivate good will, and they were some of the first that I shared with children. But when I moved from working exclusively with older children to working with four-year-olds, I needed to find a name for them that described what we were doing in a way that very young children could relate to and understand. I turned to early-child-care educator Gay Macdonald, who has over twenty-five years of experience teaching preschool children and has approximately 350 children in her charge every year in the five early-child-care facilities at UCLA. She suggested I talk about loving-kindness in the context of friendship. From that conversation, the practice of *sending friendly wishes* was born.

There are opportunities for friendly wishes practices hidden in every aspect of life, and they are limited only by your imagination. Teachers and parents I've worked with have woven friendly wishes into everyday activities, inspired by swimming pools, rock concerts, and quiet secluded forests. I encourage you to look to the people, places, pets, and other living things that have been meaningful in your lives and use those memories as silk ribbon from which you can weave your own friendly wishes. To help get you started, here's a general framework inspired by classical loving-kindness practice, but modified for young children whose minds, due to their developmental stage, may still struggle with abstract concepts.

- Ask your children to send friendly wishes to themselves, imaging that they are happy and having fun, that they're healthy, and that they're safe with their family and friends.
- Next, suggest they choose a friend or family member, hopefully someone in the room with them, and silently send

friendly wishes specifically tailored for that person. For example: "Daddy, I want you to be happy; I hope all your dreams come true; I want you to be healthy and strong; I want you to feel lots of love in your life; I want you to get home from work early so you can play with me; I hope you feel peaceful and calm; I want you to be safe always."

- After sending friendly wishes to someone they know, preferably someone in the room with them, suggest they send friendly wishes to people who aren't in the room, starting with their family and friends, then moving to people they've met, those they haven't met yet but would like to meet, and finally all living things in the whole wide world. The children might imagine themselves saying to these people, places, and living things: "I hope you're happy; I hope that you're healthy and have a lot of fun, that you're safe and never get hurt, and that you live in peace with people you love."

- Older children and teens can send friendly wishes to people who annoy them or who are having a difficult time. I steer clear of these practices with young children, though.

- With young children, I close the circle of friendly wishes with the children themselves, by asking the children to internalize them again and say to themselves silently, "May I be happy, may I be healthy and strong, may I be cozy, safe, and living in peace with my family, my friends, my pets, and all those I love."

Friendly wishes is one of several practices that can lead children toward experiencing beginner's mind. Another is mindfulness of breathing.

Breathe In . . . Breathe Out

Most of us can pinpoint a time when we found ourselves in a transcendent mental state, or beginner's mind. These experiences can come out of nowhere and be so powerful that they are life changing. Imagine training your mind so that you are better able to access this mental state anytime and anywhere you choose. Relatively few have mastered this skill completely, but the training to build the mental capacity to do so is remarkably straightforward, even simple. It's as simple as breathing.

An untrained mind has been compared to a wild elephant that chases through the forest and tears up everything in its wake. A wild elephant has enormous potential for good, but the challenge is to train it. The classic image for training a wild elephant is to tether it to a post. At first, the elephant will pull and try to get free, but the tether keeps it secured. Eventually, it will realize the effort is fruitless, and stand peacefully. When first learning mindfulness of breathing, an untrained mind wanders from thought to thought, and from one story to another, just like a wild elephant that tries to wander away from the post. The post in breath awareness practice is the physical act of breathing, and the tether is mindfulness, that gently brings our attention back to the breath. Like an elephant tied to a post, our minds and bodies will settle peacefully when we practice mindful breathing, if we are patient and give ourselves the time and space for it to occur.

Practicing mindful breathing, we feel what's happening in our minds and bodies as we rest in the sensation of our breath. There's no right or wrong way to breathe; long breaths are no better than short ones, deep breaths no better than shallow ones. Nor is there a need to do anything special; the aim is to fully experience what it's like to be alive right now, in this present moment. Give it a try, first by yourself and then, both you and your children together. There's a classic teaching that parents, even those well versed in mindfulness, often forget: *When you protect yourself, you protect others. When you protect others, you protect yourself.*[3] Parents are notorious for putting the needs of everyone else in the family before their own. Despite our good intentions, it's possible to miss the connection between taking care of our families and taking care of ourselves. To paraphrase a great mindfulness teacher, "If you are sunk in the mud, you cannot help others out of it.

"So, before practicing breath awareness with your child try it on your own to see the benefits in your own life. Once you have an understanding of mindful breathing, you'll be able to teach your child." But first, you and your children need to find a comfortable, seated meditation posture.

CRISSCROSS APPLESAUCE

Imagine a three-legged stool with its weight resting evenly on each leg. That's the idea behind a pose that kids call crisscross applesauce, in which you sit cross-legged on a pillow, one leg over the other, with weight distributed evenly between your two knees and bottom. In crisscross applesauce your back is straight and your eyes are closed or softly focused downward. In some traditions this soft downward gaze is called "modesty of the eyes." If it's difficult to sit crossed-legged on the floor, there are less strenuous and equally stable positions, including kneeling on a cushion or meditation bench and sitting on a chair with back straight and feet flat on the floor next to each other.

Kids sometimes slouch down while meditating, and sometimes their bodies will tense when they sit up straight. To help children find a relaxed and upright posture, try Zipping Yourselves Up. Do this together by imagining you have a zipper running up the middle of your body, starting at the belly button and ending just below the chin. With one hand held in front of the torso, near the belly button but not touching it, and the other hand behind the torso, near the base of the spine but not touching it, move your hands along your spine and chest and over your chin while saying "Ziiiiiiiiiiip!" Now that you're all zipped up, with your hands stretched high about your head and reaching for the sky, give a *silent* cheer, by waving your hands without saying a word. Then drop your arms back down and start all over again, with the other hand in front and the other hand in back. Zip up and cheer again silently before you drop your hands back down to rest easily on your knees.

In this centered and comfortable posture, you and your children are ready to focus your attention on the feeling of your breathing as your breath moves in and out of your bodies.

BREATH AWARENESS PRACTICE

At the beginning of each meditation period, release as much physical tension as possible in order to rest in a feeling of ease and spaciousness. Relax your body and your mind, and without great effort or expectation, let your mind settle in its natural state—open, clear, and expansive—as you give both body and mind an opportunity to rest. Regardless of where you are now and what you have to do later, in this moment the only thing to do is meditate and rest. There's no place else you need to go. There's nothing else you need to do. There's no one else you need to please. Right now, nothing is more important than taking care of yourself. So, for just a few minutes, give yourself a break. Feel the sensation of your breath as it is right now, without manipulating it in any way. Maybe your breath is slow and steady. Maybe it is quick and short. Maybe it's regular; maybe it isn't. It doesn't matter one way or the other. All that matters is that you pay attention to how it feels, without analyzing it, without doing anything at all other than resting in the experience of breathing and being alive.

Don't be concerned if either you or your children feel physically uncomfortable the first few times you focus on your breathing in this way. It's not uncommon for kids to feel as if their breathing is constricted, or to recognize for the first time that they breathe through their mouths rather than their noses and don't like the way that feels. Nor is it uncommon for an unpleasant or difficult emotion to come up right away. All of this is perfectly natural. Just encourage the children to notice the feeling and put aside analyzing it until later. Here's how I explain this to my students; you can put it in your own words when you describe it to your kids:

EXPLAINING BREATH AWARENESS TO CHILDREN

A funny thing happens to me when I observe my breath, and maybe it happens to you, too. Just observing it, without doing anything, can change the way I breathe. Often just by noticing my breath, it becomes deeper and slower, and the space between the in breath and the out breath grows longer. That's pretty amazing! Then something else happens. As my breath begins to slow and deepen, my body and mind begin to feel differently. When my breath becomes slower and quieter, and I am able to concentrate on it to the exclusion of all else, my body tends to relax, and as my body relaxes, I often feel my mind slow down and quiet.

But sometimes I simply can't concentrate on my breath without getting distracted by what I'm thinking or feeling. My mind doesn't slow down, and my body doesn't relax. In fact, the opposite happens. If I'm worried about something and can't concentrate, my breath may become short and fast, and my body may feel the way it feels when I'm worried or upset. If this happens to you, too, don't worry; it's completely natural and makes a lot of sense, given that you're thinking about something that bothers you. When you're thinking about something upsetting, you're not concentrating on your breath but on something else. So once you recognize you're thinking about your problems, gently shift your attention back to the breath and see if you start to feel better. That moment, noticing that you're distracted before shifting your attention back to your breath, actually is a moment of mindful awareness.

Before I practice mindfulness of breathing with young children, I talk to them about how breath, body, and mind tend to change when we pay attention to our breathing in this way. When working with older kids and teens, I don't describe the process. Instead, we practice together and then I ask them questions that will hopefully lead them to recognize their own processes. For example, I'll ask teens and older children, How was your first breath awareness practice? Did you keep your mind on your breath? Did your breath change as you practiced? This encourages them to look inward first for the answers and then to trust their own understanding of what happened.

I recently asked an eight-year-old student named Carey about his meditation practice. When we started working together, he couldn't sit still for any length of time, nor was he able to contain his thoughts. Carey needed to express whatever thoughts came up, whenever they came up. I worked with him twice a week over a three-week period, and by the sixth session he said, "When I am angry, my breath is strong like a lion. When I am excited, my breath is like a squirrel running around. When I am sleepy, my breath is slow like a turtle." Here's a kid who understands how his breath relates to different mind and body states.

Generally, when we practice mindfulness of breathing, we rest in the ordinary rising and falling of the breath without doing anything special to it. As we settle into our breathing, we notice the changes that naturally occur in our bodies and minds. Just like Carey, we begin to understand that different ways of breathing affect our minds and bodies. Sometimes kids need help seeing these connections, and even those who can make connections on their own sometimes take a long time to figure them out. You can speed up the process by having children breathe slowly or quickly and ask them to make connections between how they breathe and what happens in their minds and bodies. Usually kids feel more calm when they breathe slowly than they do when they breathe quickly, but not always. Without a practice like this one pointing kids toward an association between breath, body, and mind, it can be tough for kids to connect the three. It's especially difficult, if not impossible, for very young children to make this connection, so don't push them beyond their ability level. With that in mind, here's an exercise appropriate to try with kids at any age.

MAKING CONNECTIONS BETWEEN BREATH, BODY, AND MIND

Check in to see how your mind and body feel now. Take three deep breaths, and check in with your mind and body again. Anything change? Consider three separate parts of breathing: the inhalation, the exhalation, and the pause between the two. Let's notice each of these three parts of the breath and see what happens. Sitting comfortably, we're going to pay attention to absolutely everything about our breathing.

1. First, let's feel what it's like when our breaths are long. Take a long breath in and a long breath out. Pay attention to everything about your long inhalation. Now pay attention to everything about your long exhalation. How does it feel? Where do you feel it in your body? Is it fast?

Is it slow? Is it cool? Is it warm? Is it smooth? Is it rough? Is it steady? Notice how your body is feeling right now. Does your body feel any different than it did before? How? Where? In your head, your stomach, your shoulders, your neck?

2. Next, we are going to notice what it feels like when our breaths are short. Take a short breath in and a short breath out. Pay attention to everything about your short inhalation. Now pay attention to everything about your short exhalation. How does it feel? Where do you feel it in your body? Is it fast? Is it slow? Is it cool? Is it warm? Is it smooth? Is it rough? Is it steady? Notice how you are feeling right now. Does your body feel the same when you take long breaths as it does when you take short breaths? If not, what's different about it? Where do you feel the differences? In your shoulders? Your neck? Your back?

3. Now, breathe naturally. Pay attention to the inhalation, the exhalation, and the space between. Notice the beginning and the end of each inhale and each exhale. Can you rest in the space between the two, extending it for just a moment? How does that feel? Does anything change in your mind and your body? Do any parts of your body feel differently than they did before?

4. Let the feeling of your breathing fade into the background as you shift your attention from your breath to your body as a whole. How do your arms feel? Your legs? Your stomach? Your forehead? Your shoulders? Are you hungry? Cold? Warm? Relaxed? Tense? When you change the way you breathe, does the way your body feels change, too?

5. Now, use your breath to help you slow down and relax. Breathe in and let your muscles relax. Breathe out and let go of any tension in your mind and body. Breathe in and let your muscles relax. Breathe out and let go of any tension. Breathe in, relax. Breathe out, rest. Breathe in, relax. Breathe out, rest.

Breath Awareness
While Moving and Lying Down

There are people who find sitting still to practice mindfulness difficult, if not impossible, and they can practice breath awareness while moving or lying down. Practicing mindfulness of breathing while lying down is a useful bedtime routine, and it also works well before rest time in school. Because children lie still for a relatively long period of time, it's helpful to begin with a stretch. Any stretching activity from dance or yoga will do the trick. I like the Starfish Stretch because it combines breath awareness with stretching.

STARFISH STRETCH

Before beginning this stretch, I talk to kids about how starfish have five limbs that come together in the center of their bodies. Almost everything a starfish does starts from its center. Starfish eat from their centers and their movements start from their centers. We talk about how people do a lot from our centers, too. We even breathe from our centers. Then, everyone finds a place on the floor where they are able to lie on their backs and stretch their arms and legs out to the sides like a starfish, without touching anyone else. We imagine that our two arms, two legs, and heads (including our necks) are the five limbs of the starfish. While taking a deep breath into our abdomens (or our centers), we stretch all five limbs out against the floor like a starfish, imagining that the movement starts in our middles and spreads out through our arms, legs, necks, and chests into our hands, feet, and heads. After stretching as we inhale, we exhale and relax, resting our bodies against the floor—arms, legs, back, hands, feet, necks, and heads. Then we stretch our five limbs (including our heads and necks) again, while breathing in. When we breathe out, we relax and let any tension that we held in our bodies fall into the floor and the earth below.

We repeat the Starfish Stretch a few times before we sink into a still pose, letting the weight of our bodies relax into the floor. Now we're ready to rest and rock our stuffed animals to sleep.

ROCKING A STUFFED ANIMAL TO SLEEP WITH YOUR BREATHING

Ask your children to lie still on their backs with their legs flat on the floor (or mattress), arms by their sides and, if they are comfortable doing so, with their eyes closed. Once the children are comfortable, encourage them to let the weight of their bodies drop into the floor or mattress below them and relax. Then you place a stuffed animal on each of their abdomens. Use your own words when guiding them through this exercise, but if it's helpful I offer this example of what I might say:

See if you can relax and feel your head against the pillow. Your back against the floor. Your arms by your sides. Feel the weight of the stuffed animal on your belly. Now imagine that you're giving the animal a gentle ride with your breath: as you breathe in, your belly fills with air and the animal rocks up; as you breathe out, your belly empties and goes down. Breathing in, the animal rocks up, and breathing out, the animal rocks down. You don't have to change your breath or do anything at all, just notice how it feels as you breathe in and out. If you like to pretend your stuffed animal is real, you can pretend you're rocking it to sleep with a gentle ride on your belly as your breath moves in and out.

You may suggest any or all of the following, depending on your child's ability to comfortably lie still and quiet over an extended period of time. These instructions are similar to those I use when children practice breath awareness while sitting, but I've modified them to use with younger children when they are lying down.

- *You may notice that by paying attention to your breathing, it changes naturally; for example, it may become slower and deeper.*
- *You may notice that by paying attention to your breathing, the space between the breaths in and out lengthens.*
- *You may notice that by paying attention to your breathing, the feelings in your body change naturally; for example, your body may feel more calm and relaxed.*

- *You may notice that as your breath becomes slower and deeper, it becomes easier to lie still, and your mind may naturally slow down and become quieter as well.*

- *You may notice that as everyone in the room slows down and notices their breathing, the atmosphere in the room shifts and feels a bit different. Maybe it becomes easier to rest and pretend you're rocking your stuffed animal to sleep.*

- *You may notice that it helps you pay attention when your friends, your siblings, and your parents are paying attention in the same way, too. That's teamwork, and it's what happens when we all work together.*

At the end of this practice I invite children to silently send friendly wishes, if they are still awake. To prompt them you can quietly voice aspirations that are meaningful to you and your family. For example,

First ask your children to send friendly wishes to themselves: *"May I be happy; may I be healthy and have lots of fun; may I be safe and strong; may I live in peace with my family and people I love . . ."* Then to others: *"May everyone be happy; may everyone have people in their lives who they love. I want everyone in the world to have a home where they feel cozy and safe; I hope that everyone is healthy and has lots of good food to eat; I wish that everyone in the whole wide world could live together in peace."* And they can send friendly wishes to the stuffed animals that they're pretending to rock to sleep: *"Let's pretend that your stuffed animal has real feelings and it loves to rock up and down on your belly as you breathe. Let's put our hands on the stuffed animal and give them a little pat. Imagine we're telling them, 'I hope you're happy; I hope you feel love; I want you to have a peaceful life; I hope lots and lots of children play with you and send you friendly wishes.'"*

Don't be surprised if your children don't settle in quietly at first, even though they're lying down. One of my pre-K students had a tough time with this because he didn't like it when I talked about the stuffed animals as if they were real. He interrupted me repeatedly to whisper that his frog wasn't real. Every time he mentioned that the stuffed animals weren't alive, I reminded him that we were just pretending. After several minutes he seemed satisfied with my explanation and eventually found a way to calm himself by curling up in a blanket and rolling back and forth, rocking himself to sleep rather than rocking the stuffed animal. This rhythmic and repeated movement helped him relax and eventually lie still.

The utilization of rhythmic and repeated movements, like the rocking that comforted my preschool student, is commonplace in contemplative and calming activities the world over: Hasidic Jews and Tibetan monks rock forward and back while memorizing text, Native American elders rock as they chant, sports fans sway side to side in a stadium, the elderly rock in swings on their front porch, and mothers rock their babies to sleep. Noticing all the rocking and swaying across traditions, I was curious to discover what it does scientifically, so I turned to educator and dance/movement therapist Dr. Suzi Tortora, who had been my daughter's dance teacher in Garrison, New York. Tortora connected the rocking and swaying movements with two critical and sometimes overlooked sensory systems: the proprioceptive system and the vestibular system. These two sensory systems are often underdeveloped in children with developmental delays, particularly those who have challenges with sensory integration.

The proprioceptive system is the feedback system through which you know where your body is in space, both on its own and in relationship to other people and things. To get a sense of the proprioceptive system, close your eyes or look straight ahead and slowly raise one arm while paying close attention to all the sensations that accompany this movement. You know where your arm is, even though you're not looking at it, thanks to the proprioceptive system.[4] The vestibular system manages your senses of balance, equilibrium, and muscle tone. It also affects children's ability to select and maintain attention during an action. Working together, these systems allow children to feel how their bodies are contained, integrated, and physically separate from others, and appropriately place their bodies in space, in relationship to other people or objects. In other words, with increased awareness of balance and where their bodies are in space, kids better understand themselves, and are better able to control their bodies. Knowing this, it made sense to me that any movement that activated and developed these sensory systems would be useful to kids practicing mindfulness, especially for those who find it uncomfortable to sit still for an extended period of time.

Many children find it hard to sit still and meditate. The physical discomfort and extreme effort it takes for them to remain composed and quiet can be overwhelming, and so swaying side to side is helpful, and even crucial, to many when they first attempt a formal introspective practice. I adapted the Pendulum movement to help these kids, using the classical practice of walking meditation, what I call Slow and Silent Walking, as a model.

SLOW AND SILENT WALKING

There are three main movements in Slow and Silent Walking: lifting the foot, moving it forward, and placing it back down. Starting out it's helpful to narrow the focus of the activity, by paying attention to only one aspect of walking: it could be on the physical pressure on the soles of the feet when one foot steps on the ground, for example, or any other aspect of stepping. What is important is that your awareness remains on the sensory impression—the feeling of lifting, moving, and placing. After a few sessions of this exercise, students can pay attention to two aspects of walking: lifting up *and* stepping down, for example, or moving forward *and* placing the foot on the ground. Eventually, students will pay attention to all three aspects: lifting, moving, and placing. Please note that the objective of Slow and Silent Walking is not to become absorbed in the sensory experience but to become aware of how it feels and any emotional reactions that come up during your practice.

As students pay close attention to their walking, some tend to slow down automatically, while others find it difficult to slow their pace. If this happens, reverse the order of this process and encourage students to slow down first deliberately. Slow walking can be frustrating, and as with every practice when working with children, it is important to tailor it so that your children feel comfortable and enjoy practicing them.

I teach the Pendulum in a way that's similar to how I teach Slow and Silent Walking, and I substitute the side-to-side movements for those of walking. Both Slow and Silent Walking and the Pendulum are concentration exercises, with the object of attention being the sensory experience. As in all concentration practices, when the kids' minds have wandered, they should bring them back to the object of attention.

PENDULUM

The aim of this activity is to help those who find it hard to sit still to meditate in a group. To do so I help children find and establish a repetitive, rhythmic swing that *they* find soothing. Irregularly paced or shaped movements tend not to promote a sense of calm, center, and concentration. Because the Pendulum must be calming to be effective, and what is calming to one child can agitate or frustrate another, the pace and duration of each child's swing will vary. As long as children don't intentionally knock into one another, there is no right or wrong pace for the swinging motion.

I use the classical instructions for Slow and Silent Walking as a reference point when teaching the Pendulum. Just as there are three main movements (sometimes called occurrences) while walking—lifting, moving, and placing—there are three main movements in the Pendulum: moving, shifting, and finding center. Starting in a centered position either seated on a cushion, or standing, you first move (or sway) to one side, keeping your bottom on the cushion. The swaying motion is similar to moving in Slow and Silent Walking. When you reach the point at which you cannot sway any farther without lifting your bottom, shift your weight to sway back toward the center. Shifting your weight is similar to the lifting movement in Slow and Silent Walking. Once you've shifted your weight, sway back again toward the center. When you reach the center of the cushion, pause for a moment. If you feel perfectly aligned in the center of the cushion, you have found your center point. Pausing for an instant in the center is similar to the placing movement in Slow and Silent Walking. The instruction for the Pendulum goes something like this: swaying, shifting, swaying, center. Continue your side-to-side movement to the opposite side and then back to center: swaying, shifting, center, swaying, shifting, center.

At the beginning, there is a slight pause at each change, but gradually, as with Slow and Silent Walking, the practice becomes more fluid. As the students become familiar with the eight pieces of the exercise (swaying, shifting, swaying center, swaying, shifting, swaying center) and the movement becomes more fluid, you can encourage them to sway through center so that you're swaying from side to side without pause. It is helpful to use a stringed instrument to accentuate each change, strumming each time you move, pausing each time you shift. In both Slow and Silent Walking and the Pendulum, the movement can be awkward at first, when it's broken down into sections, but over time it becomes easier and the flow of the movement more natural.

Research has yet to be done into whether or not the Pendulum promotes development of the sensory systems, but practically speaking, this exercise makes it possible for children who have a difficult time sitting still to practice mindful breathing in a seated position. It's beneficial to practice in a group, and the Pendulum provides a way for children at both ends of the self-regulatory and attention spectrums to work together.

Seeing the success of the Pendulum swing, Suzi Tortora developed another fun activity to help kids understand body boundaries and posture even further, here with the aid of an imaginary bubble. Here's how I introduce it to a class.

BUBBLES IN SPACE

Kids mark their space by drawing an imaginary circle on the floor around their bodies. This circle is the boundary for an imaginary "bubble" that cannot be popped without permission and can expand to become huge—with enough space inside to hold an infinite number of people and possibilities—or contract to become very, very small. Children can stretch or shrink their bubble at will. If the room is crowded, the bubbles are small. When there is plenty of room, the bubble can be as big and wide as a child's imagination.

> *Sitting cross-legged on the floor, imagine that your bubble is enormous and reach out to feel it. Now draw your arms close to your body and imagine that your bubble gets smaller, too. Notice how your bubble changes all the time. When you are in a wide-open space, your bubble can be huge if you want it to be. When you're in a small space, like the classroom, your bubble is smaller and very close to your body. Large or small, your bubble is still there, and no one, absolutely no one, can pop it if you don't want them to.*

Every bubble is unique, and students can imagine "decorating" their bubbles with hearts, stars, Legos, reptiles, families, candy, and pretty much anything they want. Then they move around the circle and "test" one another's bubbles by pretending to bounce off the side of someone else's invisible bubble. Then, two kids "test" each other's bubbles in slow motion by bringing the palms of their hands as close to each other as possible without touching, and then the same with their arms, legs, hips, and shoulders.

The bubble practices are a fun and effective way to promote awareness of body boundaries and to develop self-regulatory skills. They're also a fantastic prelude to a game we call Tic-Toc, which is a version of the Pendulum adapted for young children.

TIC-TOC

In this exercise, children sit on a cushion or chair with their eyes closed or softly focused on an object—maybe a rock or drum. Begin with a wide swing from side to side to bring awareness to the feeling of their bodies moving in space. Starting from an upright, seated position, children slowly swing their bodies to the right (keeping their bottoms firmly on the cushion) and then slowly swing back through their center to the left. With young children, it's a good idea to limit the amount of time kids sway side to side

and to regulate their pace. You can set a rhythm by beating a drum; strumming a guitar, dulcimer, or other stringed instrument; or having the children
sway to the phrase, "Tic-toc, like a clock, until we find our center"—swaying right on the word *Tic*, left with *toc,* right with *like a clock,* left with *until
we find our,* and returning to settle into a visceral sense of our centers with
the word *center.*

I also use movement to help transition from one activity to another.
Following a mindfulness game, I ask kids to stand up in slow motion, paying attention to every movement. I encourage them to notice how their weight shifts; how their arms, legs, and head move;
and how their bodies feel, putting aside their thoughts for a moment. Then I suggest they do the same thing in reverse, from standing to sitting, paying close attention to the feeling of the movement
in their bodies and how those sensations shift, change, and morph
into something completely different and unexpected, all on their
own. When practicing in this way, we don't do anything special or
unusual with our bodies. We're just along for the ride, and we notice what happens naturally.

Whether moving, sitting still, or lying down, practicing mindfulness of breathing on your own—or together with your family—
is a pleasure and can be done at any time of the day or night. It's not
necessary to sit in full lotus position to meditate, even though gor-
geous, fit people in glossy magazine ads, TV shows, and movies are
depicted doing it that way. You and your children can meditate
quite nicely sitting in a chair, or on a cushion, or walking back and
forth along a hallway. Be inspired by this classical image from the
glorious landscape of Tibet: *Body like a mountain; breath like the
wind; and mind like the sky.*

Mindfulness Together:
Discovering the Peaceful Place That Is
Already Inside of You

Many of the mindfulness activities I practice with children are derived from classical breath awareness practices for adults. But there are a number of classical practices not focused on breath awareness that can be adapted for children and teens, too. One guides us to open to our present moment experience and discover the peaceful place that's inside all of us. Here it is:

Sit comfortably in your chair and place your hands on your knees, feet flat on the floor, back straight, chin tucked, and eyes softly gazing downward or closed, whichever is most comfortable. Briefly scan your body with your attention, and if you notice any physical discomfort, adjust your posture so that you are more comfortable. If you cannot sit upright comfortably, lie flat on your back on the floor with eyes closed or gazing softly down toward your chest. Once you feel as comfortable as possible, turn your attention to the movement of breath through your body and settle into the physical sensation of breathing for a moment or two. After your body is relaxed, turn your attention to your mind.

Sometimes we can feel as if our minds are locked up in our bodies, but they are not; when we meditate, they can be as open as space. And wherever we look for our mind—legs, fingers, stomach, heart—we'll find it because the nature of mind is everywhere and nowhere at the same time.

If this way of viewing the mind doesn't resonate with you, there are other, more concrete, ways to visualize it. One is to view the mind as a force of nature, like the sky, an ocean, or a river. Picture the sky on a late summer afternoon, just before sunset, on a day when there are no clouds. When you look into the great expanse of the sky above, you see the setting sun and a vast palette of colors: pinks, oranges, blues, purples. The mind in its natural state can be a little bit like that.

When we look up and see the sky, we know that it's there, and we understand what it is. But we can't touch it. Nor can we identify just one place where it resides. We cannot always conceptualize a force of nature nor accurately break it down into component parts. As Alan Watts writes in *The Watercourse Way,* "There is no way of putting a stream in a bucket or the wind in a bag."[5] Like the rivers, the wind, and the sky, the mind is also a manifestation of nature and cannot be separated from the whole. It is not found in a single place. It's not locked up in our hearts or in our heads. It doesn't start at one point and stop at another. Here is a way to begin a meditation using this imagery:

Let's relax our bodies, let's relax our minds, and without great effort or expectation, let our minds settle. Let's allow our minds to be open, expansive, and rich with color, like a summer sky at sunset, as we give both our bodies and our minds an opportunity to rest in their natural state.

Chapter 4

Refined Awareness:

Learn How to Pay Attention

I wish I was smart.
I wish my family was nice
I wish my mom was happy
I wish my family would be happy
I wish my family would travel
I wish me and my family could be happy.

Sixth-grade student

The first time Jessica came into my office, she sat down on a cushion in full lotus position, legs crossed over one another like a pretzel. Her eyes were closed and her palms faced upward, thumbs and middle fingers touching in a classical hand gesture called a mudra. The full lotus posture and mudra is often seen on TV and in magazines, but it can be difficult to hold, and it distracts many children from mindfulness of breathing. I sat on the floor next to her and suggested she concentrate on feeling the movement of her breath to the exclusion of all else. I sensed that her mind was somewhere else and asked, "Where's your attention? What are you concentrating on *right now*?" Jessica thought for a second and told me that she was thinking about keeping her thumb and middle finger touching each other. She was paying attention to her posture rather than her breath, which was no better or worse than paying attention to her breathing so long as she was aware of it. So we shifted gears from breath awareness to meta-awareness and began our first lesson on paying attention to what we pay attention to and how.

Attention: It's Not What You Think

Do you remember a time when you first became aware of something, before you put words to the concept? Maybe it was when you realized that someone was approaching you but you were not yet sure who, or perhaps it was a flash of awareness just before you were able to verbalize an idea. Kids inhabit this mental space much of the time. There is remarkable clarity in these brief moments of nonverbal, nonreactive awareness, as well as a sense of wonder, possibility, and mystery that is difficult to put into words. These mental impressions, called bare attention, are ethically neutral[1] or, to use the vocabulary of Jon Kabat-Zinn's mindfulness-based stress reduction, nonjudgmental,[2] but they can nonetheless create a positive shift in a child's perspective. With training and practice, people can learn to extend these brief, neutral impressions for longer than a fleeting moment and to piece them together one by one until they gradually develop a capacity to sustain longer and longer periods of nonreactive awareness. Armed with this perspective, they learn to relax and feel what is happening, as it is happening, without reacting to it. This mindful perspective is clearheaded and curious, free from preconceived notions that often dictate how people live.

Just as we have to learn to walk before we can run, and add before we can solve algebra problems, the capacity to attend in this way evolves over time and with practice. Sometimes strong, stable attention skills come naturally, but not always, and in schools where having and maintaining a strong focus is necessary for success, underdeveloped attention skills can be an enormous impediment to learning. In these highly goal-oriented environments, there's little to no room for kids whose attention needs development. Mindful-ness teacher Gene Lushtak, who taught with me for a year in Los Angeles, confessed at an early conference on mindfulness and edu-cation, "When I was a kid, adults were always telling me to pay at-tention. No matter how hard I tried, I didn't get it. I just didn't understand, until I started working with children myself and real-ized that we don't teach them how! No wonder I had so much trou-ble in my own childhood."

Teaching kids how to pay attention is important, but first, let's examine the larger, often overlooked question; When we tell kids to "pay attention!" what exactly are we asking them to do? Are we ask-ing them to focus on one thing to the exclusion of all else? Or are we asking kids to notice several things, maybe a thought, an emo-tion, and a physical sensation, all at the same time? Or would we really like them to shift their attention back and forth between one thing and another? In her book *Distracted*, Maggie Jackson writes about Dr. Leanne Tamm, an assistant professor of psychiatry at the Southwestern Medical Center of the University of Texas, who ex-plains that, when telling kids about attention, "one of the most crit-ical elements is giving kids a common language for what it means to pay attention."[3] In order to do so, we must ourselves better un-derstand that there are different types of attention and different ways of attending. Then we will be equipped to teach them how.

Let's start our discussion of attention and how it operates from the perspective of two highly rigorous disciplines devoted to the study of the mind: contemplative practice and the newer field of neuroscience.

In the world of attention research, neuroscientist Dr. Michael Posner is a rock star. Posner has spent his professional life studying attention, and while not every scientist agrees with his construct of how attention works,[4] no one can deny his influence in the field or the enormous impact of his work on its evolution. In *Distracted*, Maggie Jackson writes, "By giving us the framework and tools for decoding the enigma of attention, Posner has offered us the means for both understanding and shaping ourselves."[5] What we think of as "attention" is, according to Posner's vision, a complex system made up of three primary attentional networks,[6] each of which is shaped by experience and can be strengthened through training.[7] They are the alerting network, responsible for achieving and maintaining an alert mental state that is ready to process information efficiently; the orienting network, which orients a person's attention toward sensory events; and the executive network, which is central to the regulation of both emotions and cognition (thinking). The executive network, sometimes called executive function, enables a child to exert conscious control of her own behavior and to resolve conflict.[8] In their 2007 article on the theoretical foundations of mindfulness and evidence for its salutary effects, professors Kirk Warren Brown, Richard M. Ryan, and J. David Creswell write that early research indicates mindfulness may be linked to these three primary attention networks.[9]

Remarkable advances in neuro-imaging technologies made it possible for Posner to develop a groundbreaking body of work studying attention from the outside in, by using fMRI (functional magnetic resonance imaging) to take movies of the human brain as it works. Meanwhile, Dr. Alan Wallace was studying attention from the inside out through a classical meditation practice known as *shamatha*. The aim of *shamatha* is to develop a high degree of attentional balance and stability through a sequential, ten-stage training process. In his book *The Attention Revolution*, Wallace writes, "The stages start with a mind that cannot focus for more than a few seconds and culminate in a state of sublime stability and vividness that can be sustained for hours."[10] Mindfulness of breathing yields substantial benefits in addition to attentional stability, but a prerequisite to experiencing those benefits is the development of a strong, stable faculty of attention. Wallace is fond of quoting American philosopher and pioneer of modern psychology William James, who wrote, "The capacity to voluntarily bring back a wandering attention, over and over again, is the very root of judgment character and will."[11] Wallace's love for classical attention training is evident in every conversation, as he characterizes attention as sweet, profound, and the very essence of character and personality.

When children learn that their brains change every time they try to pay attention, they begin to make connections between effort and outcome. If they play video games all day and ignore math class, their grades may tumble. If they're helpful at home or at school, their friends and family are more likely to respond in a positive way. By making these connections, children better understand the importance of carefully choosing where they devote time and attention. I've seen dramatic, meaningful shifts in children's, especially teenagers', attitudes once they recognize that by *choosing* how to pay attention, and what to pay attention to, they are exercising their brains and changing them in a specific way. Where and how children choose to direct their attention makes a huge difference in who they are and who they will become. Truly appreciating this basic fact of life (as a child or an adult) is no small accomplishment, and it's one that's crucial to impart to children. I've watched in wonder as children have realized their own power to shape their brains and their destinies for the better. In the next section, I'll share some ways to make the science of attention understandable to kids.

Direct, Focused Attention

The first type of attention developed in classical practice is nonreactive attention directed toward a chosen object, otherwise known as focused, direct attention. When describing focused attention to kids, I compare it to archery, a sport in which the object is to hit, using a bow and arrow, a bull's-eye placed in the middle of a target. The arrow represents attention, and the bull's-eye represents children's chosen object, maybe their breath, a book, or a game. Children aim their attention and take their best shot. Just like shooting at a bull's-eye with a bow and arrow, sometimes they'll miss the target entirely and sometimes they'll hit it dead on.

Focused attention is related to the selective function of attention as children narrow their field of awareness to a specific goal. Wallace describes it as "simply being able to place your mind on your chosen object of meditation for even a second or two."[12] As in the sport of archery, when training attention, both hitting and missing the metaphorical bull's-eye are parts of the learning process. No matter how lousy a shot kids are at first, with time, practice, and motivation, their skills will improve.

After children aim their attention at a chosen object, their next hurdle is to keep it there for an extended period of time. This means they must develop the capacity to monitor where their attention is focused, detect if they are distracted, and when they are distracted, disengage their attention from the source in order to redirect and engage it back toward the chosen object of attention. In mindfulness of breathing, aiming is relatively easy, but sustaining or holding attention on the breath can be hard. Holding and refining attention on the entire circuit of breathing from the tip of the nose, through the body, and back out again is an ambitious undertaking, regardless of age. But it is particularly ambitious for young children and completely out of reach for some, unless you start with half a breath (either the inhale or the exhale) instead of a whole breath. The basic instruction is straightforward:

AIMING AND SUSTAINING

Starting with the inhalation, aim your attention on the sensation of the movement of air as you breathe in, and keep it there for half a breath, until the pause between the in and out breaths. Then reverse the process, aim your awareness on the sensation of movement of breath as you breathe out, and keep it there throughout your exhalation. Don't forget to let your body relax and notice the pause between the inhale and exhale, and then again the pause between the exhale and the inhale. Don't worry if you get distracted—you can always start over again.

With very young children, I practice breath awareness in a playful way, by blowing on colorful pinwheels and watching them spin.

PINWHEELS

There are several variations to this activity, each highlighting a specific quality of the breath. First, take a deep breath in through the nose and blow on the pinwheel with the mouth, inviting children to pay attention to how their bodies feel taking long breaths. In the second variation, children take short breaths in through the nose and blow short breaths out through their mouth to spin the pinwheel again, paying attention to how their bodies feel. It's fun for kids to watch the pinwheels spin as they notice what taking long and short breaths feels like to them.

After practicing breath awareness, whether blowing on pinwheels or sitting quietly to sense the movement of their breath, I ask children to describe what happens in their minds and bodies. They can do this with words and pictures, and over the years kids have drawn pictures of everything from angels to clouds to stars. One child wrote on the bottom of her drawing, "It feels like if you were with the angels." Another wrote, "I am doing a snow angel in the clouds." A third wrote, "I felt like a cloud in the sky."

Over the course of a day kids practice this process of aiming and sustaining attention many times—when reading a book, listening to music, or playing a sport, for example. In mindfulness we shine a light on this natural, often automatic process in order to use it deliberately. Given the vast array of aches, pains, sights, sounds, tastes, smells, and everything else that our minds process every moment, it can be difficult for children to narrow their focus and concentrate on one thing. It takes a significant amount of mental discipline to wisely choose an object of concentration, filter out peripheral sensory input, aim attention on that object, sustain it, and refine it. Regardless of age, it can be challenging to settle into breath awareness without distraction. But there are some well-established techniques that help even the most distractible minds settle. One of them is to harness the thinking mind by counting breaths. Thinking is rarely your ally when practicing meditation, but counting breaths is an exception to that rule. Alan Wallace likens it to using training wheels when first learning to ride a bicycle.[13] Counting occupies the thinking mind with a simple activity, narrowing focus with relatively little mental effort. There are several different ways to mindfully count breaths. Here are some to practice at home:

Counting Breaths

- *Counting 1-1-1-1-1-1.* When you breathe in, let your body relax. When you breathe out, silently count one, one, one, one, until your lungs feel empty. Repeat by relaxing again as you inhale and silently counting two, two, two, two, two, as you exhale. Repeat once more by relaxing as you inhale again and silently counting three, three, three, three, for the entire out-breath. Continue this exercise in sets of three breaths (counting 1 on the first exhale, 2 on the second, and 3 on the third) until your mind quiets and you can rest in the physical sensation of breathing without counting.

- *Holding a Number in Your Mind.* Another way to count breaths is to think of the number "one" and hold it in your mind as you exhale. Relax as you inhale, and as you exhale think of the number "one" and hold it in your mind for the entire out-breath. In other words, silently extend the word "one" from the beginning of the out breath to the end. With the second breath you once again relax as you inhale, and keep the number "two" in your mind throughout the exhale until your lungs feel empty. Repeat, relaxing again on the in-breath and holding the number "three" in your mind for the entire out-breath. Repeat this three-breath sequence until your mind quiets and you can rest in the physical sensation of breathing without counting.

- *Counting from One to Ten on the Exhale.* For older children, teens, and adults it can be helpful to count from one to ten on the exhalation (you'll have to count pretty quickly). Again, you relax as you inhale and count from one to ten as you exhale. Repeat until your mind quiets and you can rest in the physical sensation of breathing without counting. Some people find that counting from one to ten promotes more thinking than other counting tools. Others find the opposite to be true. That's one reason why it's important for each child to try different counting tools to see which ones (if any) help him or her.

People respond to each of these counting tools in different ways at different times, so I encourage everyone to try all three. Sometimes counting to ten will work; other times silently repeating "one" does. Look out for those who hold their breath or interfere with their normal way of breathing while counting breaths. In this practice, how quickly children count should not affect the pace of their breathing. The breath dictates the pace of the count, not the other way around. Also, make sure kids don't tense their muscles during this exercise, in their determination to keep their minds focused. Physical and mental ease are important when practicing breath awareness. It doesn't help much to be focused if kids are tense and uptight. The aim is to be focused and relaxed in mind and body.

Counting breaths is a bit advanced for very young children, but luckily, there are straightforward ways to develop breath awareness that are suitable for all ages, even preschool-age children. One is a game that can be played with one or more children called Sound in Space. The object is to settle into the feeling of breathing before listening to the sound of a tone. When the sound stops, children raise their hands. When playing this game with very young children, I demonstrate first by striking and muting the bell so that they know how it sounds when the sound starts and when it stops.

SOUND IN SPACE GAME

To begin the game, place a smooth stone, about the size of a child's palm, in front of every person in the group. I call these stones "focus rocks" and invite children to use markers to decorate them with words that are meaningful, for instance, *calm, kind, happy, joy, focus, peace, safe,* and *health.* For young children who can read but cannot yet write legibly, I write the words on the rocks myself. Kids of all ages can also decorate their rocks

with pictures and stickers. (Focus rocks can distract and could be dangerous for very young children and shouldn't be used with them.)

Next, with hands on bellies to feel the movement of the breath in the
body, lead the children through the following sequence: "Breathe with
hands on belly, look at your focus rocks, and listen for the sound of the
tone." After striking the tone, remind the children to listen to the sound as
it fades and to raise their hand when it stops. I repeat this activity three
times, or until the children begin to get bored or restless. Within a single
session, parents often notice that a child's interest and capacity to listen
increases with every round of the game. To make this game even more interesting, ask kids where the sound goes when it disappears. You will hear
some thoughtful and creative responses.

Shape Your Brain

To teach mindfulness to children, it helps to know a little about the
how the brain works. The brain is malleable, like plastic, and is
molded by repeated experiences, both inner and outer, like reading,
hearing a new language, or learning a new motor skill. The more we
engage in specific activities, the more the brain regions responsible
for these tasks organize and become functionally "healthy." And the
younger we are, the more quickly they change. This is one reason
why early childhood experience is important to brain development,
making it crucial for children to be exposed to consistent, predictable, and enriching experiences so that they develop the neurobio-
logical capabilities for health, happiness, productivity, and creativity.

Neuroplasticity, or the changeability of the physical and cellular
structure of the brain, means that our brain rewires itself in response to inner and outer life experience. *Self-directed neuroplasticity,* a term coined by UCLA researcher and clinical psychiatrist
Dr. Jeffrey Schwartz, is the process by which we can willfully cause
these brain adaptations by using our minds to change our brains. A
scientist and clinician, Schwartz also has practiced mindfulness and
studied classical contemplative texts for over thirty years.

Schwartz is one of the first to have applied mindfulness in a clinical context, in a way that is authentic and consistent with classical practice. He translated mindfulness training from the all-encompassing way it was originally practiced, as training for monks, into a highly successful mindfulness-based treatment for people with obsessive compulsive disorder (OCD). His work is ground-breaking and has helped countless people who suffer from OCD. OCD is caused by a biochemical imbalance in the brain that causes painful thoughts to intrude ceaselessly into sufferers' minds and leads them to engage in repetitive and compulsive behaviors in order to avert some imagined catastrophe. They are often preoccupied with repetitive behaviors such as washing, cleaning, counting, or checking, to the extent that it disrupts their lives.[14] With training in mindful awareness, OCD patients recognize that the intrusive messages that flood their minds can be false, and Schwartz's mindfulness-based treatment gives them specific tools to manage better with these intrusive thoughts.

In research on Schwartz's program, brain imaging verified the patients' self-reported improvement. Furthermore, Schwartz and his colleagues learned from brain scans that not only did the brain change in accordance with the improvements in his patients' functioning, but also that close attention to something, to anything, creates an attentional state that triggers self-directed neuroplasticity—not just for OCD patients but for every adult. His work showed that an intangible, volitional effort can change the physical brain. Schwartz's study was the first in a now-growing body of research that links intentionality to alterations in brain function and structure. With its focus on deliberate effort as opposed to outcome, this research could have meaningful applications for children, especially those with attention deficits. Keeping in mind the importance of introducing mindfulness to children gently, imagine helping a child develop a strong, stable faculty of attention by just encouraging her, in a fun and playful way, to try to pay attention over and over again.

One way to think about the brain is as a three-dimensional game of dot to dot, in which the dots represent neurons (brain cells) and the lines connecting one dot to another represent neural pathways. The lines connecting one neuron to another are forged and strengthened through life experience. To extend the analogy, think of the neural pathways as muscles and of life experience as physical exercise. Just as lifting weights makes muscles stronger, exercising neural pathways, makes them stronger, too. Here's how I describe this process to kids:

> *Our brains are changing all the time. Your brain is changing right now as you read this paragraph and mine is changing as I write it. When we see, hear, touch, or smell something, electrical impulses flow from one neuron (a type of brain cell) to another. Different parts of the brain communicate when a neuron fires an electrical impulse along a path, called a neural pathway, to another neuron. Each neuron has an average of ten thousand neural pathways linking it to other neurons. The signals sent by neurons create neural pathways in the brain, and that's how a brain changes over time. When one neuron "fires," it could have an impact on thousands of other neurons located in different parts of the brain.*
>
> *Imagine walking along a pathway in the grass. The more often you walk along that path, the flatter and wider the pathway gets, and it becomes easier to walk on. This is what happens when neurons fire along a path, again and again. Similarly, every time you play guitar, for example, neurons fire along a pathway in your brain, and the more you play, the bigger the pathway gets. As the neural pathway gets stronger, so does your ability to play the guitar, which is why playing chords and scales gets easier with practice. That's what self-directed neuroplasticity—or using your mind to change your brain—is all about.*

Open, Receptive Awareness

Focus is important, but there are times when you need to maintain open and receptive attention, like when you're driving a car. Drivers' primary focus is the road, but if they pay attention only to what's in front of them and ignore the rearview mirror, they can get into a lot of trouble. They also need to monitor pedestrians on the sidewalk, garbage cans along the side of the road, and cars in the opposite lane. Parents need to keep an eye on the kids in the backseat, too. Drivers monitor everything in their wide, open awareness, but keep their attention primarily focused on what is most important at the time—and what's most important shifts from moment to moment.

When practicing open, receptive attention, children adopt an impartial and receptive stance as they monitor what comes and goes from their wide field of awareness. One of my students learned that she needed to develop her capacity for open, receptive attention the hard way. She was a straight-A student with extraordinary concentration skills, but when she took driver's ed, she discovered that her ability to rest in a wider field of attention needed some work. When driving, she became so focused on whatever she was looking at that she would inadvertently steer the car directly toward it. Without realizing it, she would steer toward a mailbox, the wrong side of the street, even a pedestrian on the side of the road—a hair-raising experience for all involved. This is a common problem known as "target fixation" and, as meditation teacher Trudy Goodman fondly notes, it illustrates the classical teaching "to that which we pay attention the mind inclines." My student decided it was time to try some mindfulness training.

DRIVING AWARENESS

On a low bookshelf in my office, I have several strings, each with five colorful Tibetan flags about two-inch square hanging from it. I've arranged the strings of flags as a quiltlike tapestry. I get them every holiday from a favorite charity and over the years have collected quite a few. I use these flags as a focal point to help children broaden their field of attention. You can use any object with a patterned design for this exercise: a checked cloth, a patterned sweater, a painting. I asked my driver's ed student to sit on the floor approximately six feet away from the flags and focus on the feeling of her breath moving through her body to the exclusion of all else. Once her attention had stabilized, which happened very quickly because her concentration skills were so strong, I invited her to gaze at just one of the flags in the middle of the tapestry and focus on it. Next I asked her to expand her view to include one or two more flags, and then add a few more, until gradually all of the flags were in her field of vision, even as her primary focus remained on the original flag in the middle. Then I asked her to include everything she was sensing at that moment, too: the sounds, smells, and physical sensations. Together, we expanded awareness from the flags to everything in the room, and then to our physical sensations, thoughts, and emotions. We rested this way until we became distracted, and then we started all over again.

Another game that builds a more inclusive range of attention is Pass the Cup, where kids pass a full cup of water between two or more people.

PASS THE CUP

Everyone sits in a circle or across from one another, with a plastic cup about two-thirds filled with water on the floor between them. One person picks up the cup and slowly passes it to the next person, and it continues around the circle. The point is to pay attention to any sounds or physical sensations that might indicate your turn to receive the cup. After the water has gone around the circle one way, the direction is reversed, and the water is slowly passed in the opposite direction.

The game is repeated, only this time the participants *keep their eyes closed.* This may seem daunting at first, but it can be done, and it makes the game a lot more fun. For older children and teens, you can make this game more challenging by passing several cups of water around simultaneously, requiring a higher level of concentration and attention from everyone in the circle. After the activity, children talk about the differences between playing with eyes open and with eyes closed, and which nonvisual cues helped them know where the cup was. The trick to this game for participants is to notice the sounds in the room and where they are coming from as the water is passed around the circle. For example, if you hear clothes rustling from someone nearby, you can be pretty sure you'll get the cup soon, or if the person with the water is laughing on the other side of the circle, that's a clue that you're not likely to get it next. The trick for facilitators is to discreetly make sounds or comments that will signal to participants the location of the cup(s).

Open, receptive awareness is different from focused concentration, not just with respect to the size of the field of attention but also in its approach to distraction. When practicing direct, focused attention, anything that comes into children's minds other than the chosen object of attention is considered a distraction, whether it's pleasant (like their mom saying it's dinnertime) or unpleasant (like the end-of-class bell ringing even though they haven't finished a math test). Thus, when children recognize they are distracted, they acknowledge the distraction, set it aside, and return to their chosen object of concentration. In contrast, with receptive awareness, children don't always turn away from events of the mind and body that could be distracting; rather, they include them in their fields of attention.

Planning, Organization, and Self-Regulation

The executive function of the brain is comparable to the role conductors play when leading an orchestra. A conductor's role is to coordinate and blend the many unique voices and different instruments to create a piece of music, cuing the musicians at the appropriate time, setting the pace of the music, and determining the tone of the piece. To perform this job well, conductors must have musical talent, but they also need the life experience and training to anticipate any unexpected events and the skills to respond to them. These skills are intrinsic to executive function.

Executive function requires the capacity to harness and organize the skills of attention, memory, inhibition, and self-regulation that the brain employs at any given moment to respond to the situation at hand, as well as any emotions we experience in response. Core executive skills include:

- Inhibitory control that allows kids to resist temptations or distractions

- Working memory that allows children to remember and use information

- Cognitive flexibility that allows children to shift their attention from one object to another and view life experience from various perspectives.

Posner uses the children's game Simon Says as an example of executive function at work.[15] When the leader says, "Simon says, put your hand on your head," and puts her hand on her head, the players easily follow instruction. And when the leader says, "Simon says, jump on one foot," everyone jumps on one foot. But when the leader doesn't say "Simon says," you're *not* supposed to do what she says, even though she does it herself. When children hear the leader say, "Put your hand on your toes," then see her reach to touch her toes, there's a cognitive conflict between what they hear and what they see that they must address. Posner explains that when children are asked to execute instructions from one source (*verbally*) while inhibiting instructions from another (*visually*), the executive attention network is called upon to sort through competing messages.

In addition to being a great way to practice mindfulness (by paying attention to outer experience, in this case other people), Simon Says is a fun and handy classroom management tool.

A growing body of research out of the Mindful Awareness Research Center (MARC) at UCLA's Semel Institute suggests that mindfulness practice is associated with the development of the executive network in teens and children as young as four. I was involved in three of these school-based, randomized control studies under the general direction of Dr. Sue Smalley, head of their research efforts in education. Dr. Lisa Flook, then a postdoctoral student, led the team of researchers. Over a period of three years, we taught one hundred sixty children ages four through nine, at three different schools, and in nine separate classrooms, in the greater LA area.

The Inner Kids program was taught in all three studies. It tracks classical mindfulness of breathing using games and activities that I adapted for young children from practices originally intended for adults. The first study took place during the 2006–07 school year and was designed as a feasibility study for pre-kindergarten age children. The second study, conducted during the 2007–08 school year, was taught in second and third grade classrooms, and the third study looked at pre-kindergarten age children again during the 2008–09 school year. In each study, I taught half-hour mindful awareness classes twice a week, for eight consecutive weeks.

The first feasibility study of forty-four preschoolers demonstrated that children as young as four can successfully participate in mindfulness meditation in a group setting,[16] dispelling doubt that preschool-age children are developmentally unable to do so. Through parent and teacher reports, the second study of second- and third-grade students demonstrated significant improvement in those with executive function deficits. The areas showing improvement were behavioral regulation, metacognition (thinking about thinking), overall executive function, and specific domains of executive function. Teachers and parents reported improvement in children's ability to shift, initiate, and monitor their attention.[17] This makes sense given that these skills are the basis of breath awareness practices where children learn to aim their attention on the feeling of movement of breath (initiate), notice when their attention has wandered (monitor), and then bring their attention back to the feeling of movement of breath (shift).[18] Drs. Smalley and Flook concluded:

> These initial findings suggest that mindfulness introduced in a general education setting is particularly beneficial for children with executive function difficulties. Children who initially showed lower levels of executive function before mindful awareness training exhibited executive function in the average range after mindfulness training.[19]

In the third study of pre-elementary-age students, teachers' reports again showed a clear effect, but this time for all students, not just those with executive function deficits. Children who took the mindfulness classes showed increased executive function, specifically working memory, as well as planning and organizational skills. Because this was a school-based study, teachers could not be blind to the groups (they knew who was taking the mindfulness class and who was not) so the possibility of teacher bias cannot be ruled out. Yet, there was no evidence of it in this study and, given their role in children's lives, teachers are uniquely well suited to evaluate their students' executive functioning skills.

All three studies support the introduction of mindful awareness practices in a school-based setting showing that it can be enjoyable for kids and have a positive impact on emergent meta-cognition (capacity to think about what they are thinking), self-regulation, and overall global executive control. Research into the effect of mindful awareness on young children is just beginning, and it's important to be cautious when reporting these findings. They are nonetheless intriguing, and there's reason to be optimistic that further studies centering on the practice of mindfulness with children and their families will also show benefit.

Dr. Smalley is a research geneticist who is passionate about changing the way we think about ADHD from a "medical disorder" to a human trait that, while posing challenges to those who have it, also has its strengths.[20] Her aim in studying mindfulness in education was to better understand the role of mindfulness in the development of executive function (a common problem in ADHD), particularly focusing on teens and adults with attentional challenges. Smalley and her colleague, psychiatrist Dr. Lidia Zylowska, developed a mindfulness course designed to be "ADHD friendly" and evaluated the feasibility of their program in a pilot study. The majority of participants stayed with the program and endorsed it as useful (no small thing for teens) while also reporting improvements in ADHD symptoms and attention as measured by computer task. Without a control group, they were limited in the conclusions they could draw, but results are encouraging with respect to how mindfulness practice might support aspects of attention that are compromised in those with ADHD.[21]

Advances in neuroscience, genetics, and the secular applications of meditation will define and refine our understanding of attention for years to come. A thorough discussion of attention's role in childhood development is beyond the scope of this book, but, if asked to identify what aspect most informs my work, it would be the role of gentle and deliberate effort in refining attention. As with everything else, some kids have a natural predisposition for paying attention; others do not. But regardless of talent, simply trying to pay attention is all that it takes to begin the process of refining attention. By patiently and kindly focusing on gentle effort rather than outcome, we can start kids along a path toward strong, stable attention skills.

Mindfulness Together: Use Playing, Singing, Dancing, Creating, Having Fun as a Doorway to Experiencing Mind in Its Natural State

It can be difficult for adults and children to shift from the hectic activity of daily life into a mind-set that is favorable to meditation. When working with children and teens, I precede each period of meditation with a game or activity designed to turn kids away from analyzing what's happening and toward a less conceptual experience. Singing, dancing, blowing bubbles, drumming, playing with balloons, dancing the hokey-pokey, making collages, and just plain having fun are fantastic preludes to meditation. Philosopher and author Alan Watts was known for dancing, singing, and even talking gibberish before he sat down to write and meditate. It is said that on the evening before his death, he was batting inflated balloons around the room and called out, "Oh, if I could only figure out how to do this without my body."

You can try this at home with inflated balloons or beach balls, or you can blow bubbles together. Turn up the music (sometimes I play the song "Tiny Bubbles"), then silently blow bubbles with liquid soap and wands from the drugstore—kids and adults together.

As the music plays, bat your own and one another's bubbles with your wands. When the music fades away, encourage everyone to sit down wherever they are to rest for a minute or two and feel their present moment experience. For those who like mindfulness of breathing, it's a perfect time to practice.

Chapter 5

Friendly Awareness:

Meditate, Speak, Relate, and Act Mindfully and Compassionately

I wish that I can see one of my babysitters again
I wish that my family can be nice to me
I wish that people won't tease me or make fun
I wish that I can be free forever.

Second-grade student

In all of literature there's no creature with a bigger heart than Curious George, the main character in a series of storybooks written by Hans Augusto Rey. Curious George is a chimpanzee brought from his home in Africa by the Man in the Yellow Hat to live in a big city. Meaning well though regularly testing his owner's boundaries, Curious George has resonated with kids and parents for over sixty years, and he's a good model to help children understand the open, curious way we monitor life experience when practicing mindfulness, as well as the importance of not always reacting to what we observe, at least not immediately.

Curiosity makes George an eternal enthusiast, receptive to any experience that comes his way. He doesn't ponder things before exploring them, he's neither self-critical nor judgmental, and every experience is novel. He takes life at face value and attends to the bare facts of perception as they come to him. This receptive and playful way of seeing the world, one that's not burdened by preconceived notions, is how we bring mindful awareness to what's happening in our inner and outer worlds. Researcher Dr. Scott Bishop from the University of Toronto and his colleagues describe this perspective more formally in an academic paper that proposes an operational definition of mindfulness:

> [An] orientation (to experience that) begins with making a commitment to maintain an attitude of curiosity about where the mind wanders whenever it inevitably drifts away from the breath, as well as curiosity about the different objects within one's experience at any moment. . . . It involves a conscious decision to abandon one's agenda to have a different experience and an active process of "allowing" current thoughts, feelings and sensations.[1]

When working with children and families, I compare this mind-set to watching a play. No matter how involved you become in the plot, no matter how much you care about the characters, you don't climb up on the stage to help them out of whatever mess they might be in; you stay in your seat and watch. This is similar to how we monitor the activities in our minds and bodies when we meditate. We experience them and are touched by them much in the way we experience and are touched by a play, participating in the experience without becoming enmeshed in the drama. This is an important distinction when using mindfulness to help manage difficult emotions, and one that I'll expand on later in the book, but it is out of reach for many children. Preadolescents and teenagers have an easier time understanding this distinction and using it in their lives.

The first step of the scientific method is observation, and like good scientists, when practicing mindfulness, we start by observing life experience with an open and curious mind. One activity that helps kids learn this skill is the Hello Game. It can be played in a classroom or around the dinner table. Here's how it goes.

HELLO GAME

In this simple game, we take turns turning to our neighbor to say hello, and then noting the color of his or her eyes. I first heard of this exercise from Dr. Bill Tekeshita, a learning specialist in Santa Monica, California, who used this technique with children who had trouble looking another person in the eye. I tried it and quickly saw how this technique brilliantly removes the emotional charge, and awkwardness, of making eye contact. For example, you might make eye contact with your daughter and say, "Good morning, your eyes look blue." In response, she'll say something similar, "Hi, Mom, your eyes look brown." When there are more than two people, we sit in a circle and the greeting moves from person to person until everyone has had a turn.

Notice my wording: "Your eyes *look* blue" as opposed to "Your eyes *are* blue." I phrase the greeting to reinforce the objective of observing rather than analyzing. It's common for people to disagree about eye color, and kids often disagree about mine because their color seems to depend on what I'm wearing: sometimes they look blue; other times they seem green. By saying, "Hi, Susan, your eyes *look* green," rather than, "Hi, Susan, your eyes *are* green," kids emphasize the process of observation rather than the object being observed. It's a fine point but a useful one when teaching kids about the difference between describing what they see and drawing a conclusion.

Some kids are shy, and they cover their eyes during this game. Regardless, I encourage the child who is saying hello to describe what she sees. For example: "Hi, it looks like your eyes are covered." In response, the child with her eyes covered often feels less performance anxiety, laughs, and uncovers her eyes. Young kids will come up with fanciful descriptions of their friends' eyes, too, like saying that a friend's brown eyes look "blue," or "purple," or even "polka-dotted," which can leave the brown-eyed child confused and not sure how to respond. This is a good time to remind everyone that the objective of the game is to notice and say out loud what the other person's eyes *look like* to you, which may or may not be what they *look like* to someone else, or even to the person whose eyes you are describing. Some silly answers are to be expected, but if things start getting out of hand, this is also an opportunity to remind young children that, while silly answers can be fun, this isn't the time for them, and to encourage the kids to make another choice.

The Hello Game is a favorite of Annaka Harris, who taught the Inner Kids program at Toluca Lake Elementary School in Los Angeles for two years. When speaking at a meeting about practicing mindfulness with children, she said:

> The Hello Game teaches awareness of present experience, while instilling confidence, respect, and a sense of teamwork. This exercise is interesting to follow over the course of a semester. In the beginning, when we first do the exercise, the students are very embarrassed. There's a lot of giggling, and some of them even talk about feeling scared when they make eye contact. They become so distracted by their reaction to having to make eye contact with each other that we barely make it around the circle the first few times. But by the end of the semester, they're turning, they're looking at each other, they're maintaining eye contact, for the most part without any embarrassment, and are much more confident, really listening to each other, and staying very focused in the present moment.

There are several adaptations of the Hello Game that build awareness of our bodies, minds, other people, and the planet, which will appear in later chapters.

The next step of the scientific method is to use whatever resources are available to help better understand what you see. The same holds true when practicing mindfulness. Like the scientific method, the first step is to observe through bare attention, and the second step is to understand the experience. Meditative understanding comes when kids contextualize their experience within the framework of mindfulness teachings that include impermanence, interconnection, kindness, and compassion. This understanding is sometimes called clear comprehension. In a lively correspondence between two classical scholars, Alan Wallace and monk Bhikku Bodhi, Bodhi wrote, "Only when [bare attention and clear comprehension] work together [can] right mindfulness fulfill its intended purpose."[2]

This is a complex process that even the most seasoned meditators find challenging sometimes, especially when it touches on emotional material. To provide a safe place where children and teens can speak openly about their meditative experience, and how to make sense of it in the context of their own lives, I break the process down into clear and concrete steps that they understand and can anticipate.

- Play: First we have some fun.

- Meditate: Next we practice introspection, often mindfulness of breathing while sitting, standing, walking, or lying down. As we meditate we observe our minds and bodies from the perspective of the friendly observer, with a curious, open mind as free of preconceived notions as possible. The songs, dances, games, and other activities described in the book are examples of things we do during the first two steps of this process—play and meditate.

- Share: Then we talk about what it is like to learn to meditate and how we can use what we're learning in real life. This is an opportunity to encourage kids to seek help if something comes to mind that concerns them.

- Apply: Last, we use what we learned in our daily lives, informed by an understanding of the principles of mindfulness—particularly those of impermanence, interdependence, and community service.

To help children develop meditative understanding that Bhikku Bodhi and Alan Wallace wrote about, kids talk with me, and with one another, about their experiences—the third and fourth steps of the process. As adults who choose to practice mindful awareness with kids and teens, helping them understand their meditative experience is our greatest responsibility. We support kids as they develop meditative understanding by quietly asking them questions that turn them back into their own experience. We do not give them advice, draw conclusions, or project our experience onto theirs. There are countless opportunities throughout the day to talk with your own kids and act as a sounding board for their impressions about what's happening in their minds, their bodies, and their lives. In the car on the way to school, cleaning the kitchen, reading on the couch, or after having meditated together are all opportunities for conversation; no one time is better than another.

If there are more than two of us meditating together, we sit in a circle afterward and share our stories. Although I've taken great liberties with it, the group process used in Inner Kids classes is loosely modeled after a social emotional learning class, called the Council program, that my kids took at their schools. Derivative of Native American councils and other contemplative traditions, the Council program was adapted for classroom use by Jack Zimmerman from the Ojai Foundation in California.[3] The council format is well suited to mindful awareness practice. Its four intentions—speak from the heart, listen from the heart, be lean in your speech, and be spontaneous—encourage kids to develop their own voices and trust themselves.

Breathing Room

Back to Curious George. No matter how hard he tries to stay out of trouble, George's curiosity invariably leads him into some sticky situations. He has mastered the ability to experience whatever is happening with curiosity and good-hearted motivation, but he has not yet learned to control his response. Were George to "hold off" for a moment and give himself enough breathing room to view his experience clearheadedly, he would be better able to discern the appropriate action or response. Of course, his stories would be considerably less fun.

Holding off was explained by classical scholar Analayo, in a book that merged the data from his Ph.D. research while attending University in Sri Lanka, with his meditative experience as a monk. He wrote,

> The need to distinguish clearly between a first stage of observation and a second stage of taking action is . . . an essential feature of [this] way of teaching. The simple reason for this approach is that only the preliminary step of calmly assessing a situation without immediately reacting enables one to undertake the appropriate action.[4]

In other words, as children's worldviews become more mindful, they relate and respond to others in a less reactive and more discerning way. That said, there are times when it is far more appropriate to react rather than hold off: to laugh at a joke, for example, or catch a fly ball in the outfield. Surely, if a child's hand touches a burning ember, she should pull it back immediately before thinking it through. But delaying reaction is a commonsense method for coping with more complex situations.

Mindful speech can be taught in a way that is similar to learning to respond rather than react automatically. When sitting and talking in a circle, we ask children and teens to be mindful of what they say. Much like the importance of being clear what we mean when we ask kids to pay attention, it is equally important that our meaning is clear when we ask kids to speak mindfully. A Sufi teaching called the Three Gates can be helpful, particularly when working with elementary-school-aged children. It encourages kids to ask themselves three questions before they speak: Is it true? Is it necessary? Is it kind? Carefully observing and assessing a situation before acting, or before speaking, is an important life skill. With training and practice the first part—careful observation and assessment— can take place in the blink of an eye.

Is it true?

Is it necessary?

Is it kind?

Waiting before speaking can be problematic if not skillfully employed. I teach a course with Tom Nolan, dean of students and assistant head of Crossroads High School, that combines the Council program (which is taught at Crossroads) with the Inner Kids mindful awareness program. The Three Gates is used skillfully at Crossroads Elementary School and, in response to a question from one of our adult students, Nolan cautioned group leaders that they could inadvertently use these three questions to "limit what kids share with each other in the first place." He continued:

Sometimes it's good for kids to just say what's on their minds. In council I would much prefer that people speak from the heart, and if the shadow emerges, then we deal with it. Kids of all ages (and, of course, adults) need a place to say what they are feeling, without shame or judgment. Council provides that kind of container, and the process works with the shadow, so long as the facilitator is brave and is willing to move into it.

Nolan's comment raises a larger issue about nonreactivity: it is not always in children's best interest to chew over what they do and say beforehand. To do so in every situation would rob them of their spontaneity. Few people live deliberately all the time, and I haven't met many who think it's a great idea. Upon reflection, how many of us would want our lives to be on an even keel all of the time? Would childhood even be childhood without periodic eruptions of laughter and tears? It is possible for kids to be mindful explorers and friendly observers without squelching their natural spontaneity. As parents, it's important that we model good judgment and, unless there's reason to believe otherwise, have confidence that our kids have good judgment themselves or are in the process of developing it. It's sometimes okay for kids to take off on a spur-of-the-moment adventure, and sometimes they'll make a mistake. We hope it won't be a serious one, but trial and error are both part of growing up. To borrow from Albert Einstein, "Anyone who has never made a mistake has never tried anything new." Holding off is not intended to hold children back. It is a useful skill set meant to expand children's universe by giving them a way to navigate complex situations. It is not intended to contract their universe by inhibiting their spontaneity and creativity.

The Heckler on Your Shoulder

Throughout high school my daughter had crew practice after school every day in Marina del Rey, about a forty-five-minute drive from our house during rush hour. Before she got her driver's license, I often read at the beach while waiting to take her home. One afternoon, four young girls from the local middle school pitched camp next to me. They seemed affluent and were attractive, yet their conversation was far from pretty. Two of them, whom I thought of as the "alpha girls," were ganging up on a third, the beta girl, for no apparent reason, and the fourth girl seemed detached—engaged in the conversation though she didn't say a word. I wondered whether she would shore up her social status by siding with the alpha girls, try to rescue the beta girl, or do nothing at all.

It was torture to listen to the alpha girls mock the beta girl, and just when I was about to intervene, the fourth girl told the others to lay off. When they didn't, she asked the beta girl to walk on the beach with her, leaving the others alone on their blanket without an audience and without a target. I was impressed by the fearless and compassionate stance of the fourth girl.

The remaining two girls, left on their own, turned the beam of hostility upon themselves. They were talking about a recent trip to the mall to buy bathing suits, and it was painful to hear how they hated their noses, their "fat thighs," even the sound of their own voices, as they exaggerated and then dissected every perceived flaw. I thought of a novel my husband wrote about a comedian who joked that he had a tiny heckler on his shoulder calling out insults. For all of their strengths, and they had many, these girls lacked the ability to step back, take a deep breath, and calmly see themselves as others see them. At the time I worried that it would be impossible for them to feel better about themselves unless they could silence the hecklers on their shoulders.

Boys have tiny inner hecklers, too. A devoted grandfather once brought his elementary school grandson to see me. The boy's parents and teachers wondered if he had an attention problem because he squirmed at his desk and was distracted in school. He was a young, active boy, and it didn't surprise me that he had trouble sitting still. Generations ago kids would spend more time active and outdoors; it's unsurprising that kids today struggle with sedentary school activities sometimes. When I asked the boy about school, he told me he was miserable, not because he was struggling with his schoolwork, but because he was struggling socially. Talking to him, I realized that he had turned in on himself, the victim of his own heckling. He told me he was up at night with everything that he had done or said throughout the day running through his mind. And when he wasn't paralyzed by anxiety, he tended to act out his frustration with other boys at school or on play dates, frequently involved with pushing and shoving matches on the playground. This was taking a toll on his friendships and his schoolwork. I gave him simple techniques to remind him to stop and take a breath when he felt like he might lose his temper, and he found them to be helpful. He used similar techniques when he went to bed at night to quiet his mind so he could fall asleep. But most significantly, I talked to him about being kinder to himself. His grandfather described him as the sweetest kid in the world, and I was impressed with his level of empathy for the boys he had dustups with at school, many of whom had bullied him. I hoped that he would develop the same or greater degree of compassion and understanding for himself that he had developed for other people.

Inner hecklers are remarkably creative when it comes to making kids feel awful about themselves. One of the pernicious mental traps I hear is when kids' inner hecklers expect perfection. I've never met anyone who admits to thinking it's possible to be perfect, but I've met many who act that way. If children are prone to this way of thinking (or if their parents are), kids and parents can take a strict approach to mindfulness teachings that inadvertently sends the message that, if they meditate enough, if they become mindful enough, then they can become perfect, or at least pretty close. This goal-oriented approach is a setup for kids to feel rotten about themselves, as if they don't measure up. Many kids feel that way already, and meditating can become another activity in which they expect perfection. If your children are confronted by an inner mindfulness heckler, remind them that mindfulness is gentle process, not a harsh one.

The alpha girls on the beach who seemed desperate to look like contestants on *America's Next Top Model* had held themselves up to an outrageous physical standard. I worked with a young girl who was equally hard on herself, but in a different way. She was smart, beautiful, and talented, but, though she was only in elementary school, she held herself up to such a high academic standard that the slightest criticism brought her to tears. When she was a toddler, every block she played with had to be perfectly aligned, and every adult she met had to be pleased. Any hint that something was less than perfect validated her feeling that she was somehow bad or doing something wrong. As a result, she was often anxious, and her parents wondered what, if anything, they could possibly do to help her.

The issue of perfectionism, particularly with middle and high school students, comes up frequently in my work, and it can be a complicated one to handle. In an e-mail correspondence I asked Jon Kabat-Zinn for help with this problem, and he graciously offered me some smart and practical advice that I will pass along to you:

> Tread very carefully here. To my mind, it is better not to bring up "perfect" anything or "perfection," no matter how much it figures in classical texts. I am not a translator in that sense, not knowing Pali or any other textual languages. But we never bring up the concept of "perfection" in MBSR except to say (as I do a lot) that you are "perfect as you are, including all your imperfections." That paradoxical statement leaves a lot of room for accepting the "warts and pimples" and obvious shortcomings we (and kids) attribute to ourselves, and yet nurturing what is deepest and best and most okay (and beautiful) in ourselves, which is also already present, and so not something we need to attain. That is the case no matter how you think you appear, no matter how much you weigh, no matter how badly you feel about yourself or what you have or haven't done in any given moment. Your original nature is already and always luminous, beautiful, and whole, perfectly what it is. You may not realize it in any moment, or every moment, but perhaps you can practice at least for brief moments "as if" you are already okay, already whole, already your true self. In that regard, I like to say that "the world needs all its flowers" and that we each need to realize (and make real) what flower we are. The practice of mindfulness allows us to take off the usual distorted lenses (including and perhaps especially our thoughts and reactive, destructive emotions) and see "the bare actuality of things." That is what coming to our senses means, both literally and metaphorically.

Nothing Lasts Forever

Mindful awareness practices that help kids better understand their life experiences develop a shift in perspective that often helps kids quiet their inner hecklers. For instance, it is tough to get overly attached to things that are ultimately unimportant when you view life from the perspective of impermanence. When sad and frustrated, many kids find comfort in knowing that whatever happens—be it good, bad, or neutral—things are not likely to stay that way for very long. By taking the stance of the friendly observer, a child will, over time, begin to calmly notice that everything changes. This can be reassuring, particularly to those who have recently discovered that life is not always fair. Life may not be fair today, but that doesn't mean it'll be the same tomorrow. It can be hard to wait, but it will change. Just hold on. And when children question whether there's any logic to all of this unending change, they may start noticing connections between events that seem distant from one another. They may think about how a balloon let loose in the sky could end up hurting a dolphin in the ocean, or how American soldiers risk their lives in the Middle East so that we can get the oil produced there to fill our gas tanks. Even on a planet with 6 billion people, children can see how everything is connected, though these connections are not always obvious, and sometimes take subtlety and nuance to be perceived.

Your Own Best Friend

There are times when our inner hecklers beat us up with inside information that only they could possibly know (because they are actually part of us) and no matter how well we understand the ebbs, flows, and connections of life, the world doesn't feel like a safe place. When we're scared everything feels scary, even our own minds don't feel safe. These are the moments when we need a refuge within ourselves. At times like these, visualization practices can be of comfort; they can even be transformative. But when practicing them with children and teens, there are important issues to keep in mind.

I've met children who are coping with challenges at home or at school beyond my imagination, some of which I've known about and others that I surely did not. When practicing with kids, I remind myself that I don't know everything about *my own children's* inner and outer lives, much less the inner and outer lives of other peoples' children. For this reason, I avoid certain classical visualizations, even though they may be beneficial to adults. These include:

- A statement or implication that a child or teen *should* have any feelings at all, positive or negative, about other people.

- A statement or implication that a child *should* feel forgiveness, acceptance, or compassion for someone who is physically or emotionally harming her or him.

One way to avoid these minefields is to limit visualizations of tenderness, love, and compassion to only people who the children have chosen themselves, or to large groups of people, like their friends in school or their neighborhood, or to everyone and everything else on the planet. Also, it's important to reassure kids that they are in a safe place, literally and figuratively. When leading meditation, I remind kids that I will keep my eyes open, so it's okay for them to close theirs. Even with these precautions, some children may not feel safe, and I never force anybody to participate. I encourage children who find it difficult to lie down and meditate with other people to sit up if that's easier for them. After doing everything I can to make sure the children are emotionally and physically comfortable, I invite them to carve out some time to be kind to themselves. This is a radical idea for many people. Here's how I suggest children and teenagers begin.

A RADICAL ACT OF KINDNESS

Let's lie on the floor and pay attention to what's happening in your body. How do the different parts of your body feel right now? We're not going to think about whether or not there's something about our bodies that we'd like to change. Instead, we're going to notice how it feels to lie on the floor in this room today. Our number one priority is to take good care of ourselves. Feel your head on the pillow, the crook of your neck, your shoulders on the blanket. If thoughts come to mind as you scan your body, try not to get caught up in them. Instead, return to noticing how your arms feel lying by your sides, how your back feels against the floor, the small of your back, your rear, your legs, the backs of your heels, your feet. Try not to analyze anything right now. Just observe your body and mind as if you're a friendly and impartial spectator. If you have a heckler on your shoulder, that's perfectly natural, just see if you can ignore him or her by gently bringing your attention away from your mind and back to your body. You can even whisper silently to yourself, "Not now."

Most of us are very busy, and it's hard to find time to rest and look inside. Resting and introspection often don't seem as important as the other things we do. They're really important, though, more important than many people think.

Remember, there's no place you have to go right now. There's nothing you need to do. There's no one for you to please. There's no one else you have to be. You don't need anything other than what you have right here. All we're doing now is resting. Nothing more and nothing less.

As you feel your body against the floor, pay attention to the sense that your weight is releasing or yielding to the floor and the earth below it. Imagine that you can see the tension in your body, that your tension is like a cloud of gray smoke. And feel it all leaving your body, dropping down into the floor. Then imagine it sinking into the earth below the floor. Now try again.

Remember, there's no place you have to go right now. There's nothing you need to do. There's no one for you to please. There's no one else you have to be. You don't need anything other than what you have right here. All we're doing now is resting. Nothing more and nothing less.

Now that all of the tension in your body has released into the earth below, picture your own safe place. Your safe place can be someplace you've been, someplace you haven't been but would like to visit, or an imaginary place that you conjure up yourself. Some kids tell me their safe place is their bed; for others it's their backyard or the beach; for some it's vacation with their moms and dads. Your safe place is someplace where you are happy, you feel loved, you are strong and relaxed, and you have lots of fun. Picture yourself having fun and relaxing in your safe place.

Remember, there's no place you have to go right now. There's nothing you need to do. There's no one for you to please. There's no one else you have to be. You don't need anything other than what you have right now. All we're doing now is resting. Nothing more and nothing less.

Let's move our attention to the space deep inside our chests where our hearts are. Imagine that space is glowing with warmth, and feel the warmth slowly and steadily become sweeter and larger and deeper and wider until it radiates out to warm your torso, your neck, your shoulders, arms, hands, and fingers; it warms your hips and legs all the way to the bottoms of your feet and tips of your toes. Up to the top of your head, down to the tips of your toes, your front, your back, your middle, all the way around until your body is filled with warm light. The warmth coming from inside is enormous and limitless. Let's rest in that warmth for a while.

Remember, there's no place you have to go. There's nothing you need to do. There's no one for you to please. There's no one else you have to be. You don't need anything other than what you already have right now. All we're doing is resting. Nothing more and nothing less.

A lot of us spend a whole lot of time and energy paying attention to other people. We wonder how other people feel, what they think, what they would like us to do, and how they would like us to be. It's okay that we think about other people sometimes, but we're not going to think about other people now. Right now we're going to give ourselves a break from all of the inner talk about what other people say, do, think, and feel. We're going to let go of any thoughts we have about other people right now and do something fairly radical. We're going to take good care of ourselves and rest.

Getting to know you, I've seen how much you care about your friends and how much you support one another. I've been inspired by your teamwork. Right now we're going to be as kind, and caring, and supportive of ourselves as we are of our friends.

Rest in your safe place knowing that you are complete and whole just as you are. If you don't believe it, just go with me on this one. You don't need to do anything, you don't need to change, and you don't need to be anyone else. You are complete and whole just as you are. Whether you're happy today or sad, whether there are more bad things in your life right now than there are good things. In the long run it won't matter as much as it seems to matter now. Good times and bad times are part of life, and like the tide they come and they go. One thing's for sure, they'll always change. Sometimes it's hard to wait but just hold on.

We're going to end by sending friendly wishes to ourselves. Picture yourself in your safe place where you're happy and having a lot of fun. Maybe you're singing, maybe you're dancing, maybe you're reading, maybe you're resting, maybe you're playing a guitar. Whatever you love to do, you can do in your safe place. May you be healthy and strong. May you be with people you love and who love you. Everyone in your safe place is relaxed and at ease. Everyone in your safe place is peaceful, free, and having fun.

Self-compassion practices can be difficult for both children and adults. If you are one of the many people who find these practices challenging, I encourage you to find a well-trained meditation teacher to help you with them. Early research has associated self-compassion with other positive qualities like wisdom, personal initiative, curiosity, happiness, and optimism. What's more, even if you don't feel much compassion for yourself right now, early findings and thousands of years of experience suggest that might change if you practice mindful awareness.[5]

Mindfulness Together:
Discovering the Beauty That's Always Inside

One important classical teaching is that it's tough to be happy when we don't recognize the beauty of our true nature. The image of an exquisite gem hidden beneath four veils is a lovely way to illustrate this teaching.

Take a pretty object from your cabinet or jewelry box, put it on a table, and cover it with a few scarves. Later, you can tell your children about times in your own life when you doubted your true nature, and ask your children if they can think of examples from their lives, too. With each story about a difficult experience that clouded your visions of yourselves, remove a scarf. At last, when you take away the final scarf, the hidden, beautiful object is revealed, emblematic of the beauty that lies within all of us.

Chapter 6

Sensory Awareness:

Become Aware of the

Physical World

I wish my life could be amazing
I wish my life could be happy
I wish I could do my work fast
I wish I didn't go to bad places
I wish I could be loved and kind.

Fourth-grade student

Eating is easy. Sometimes, it is way too easy, so easy that it's one of the most reflexive things we do. Every now and again I'll savor a truffle, the piquant flavor of a sweet Vidalia onion, or the bouquet of Tuscan Chianti. But all too often, I eat mindlessly while talking or thinking about something else. That changes when I practice mindful eating with my family. Mindful eating is a brilliant way to pay attention to what we hear, taste, see, smell, and touch all at the same time, and we can do it at every meal of the day.

Here's what has become the classic mindful-eating practice, which was introduced by Jack Kornfield and made famous by Jon Kabat-Zinn in his mindfulness-based stress reduction program.

With this awareness exercise, you and your kids can share a transformative experience just by eating a raisin.

EATING A RAISIN

Start by looking at a raisin, its uneven crevices, its irregular shape, and its rich brown color. Try not to analyze, just look. What's that like? Imagine the fertile earth from which the grapevine burst forth, the soft rays of the sun, and the rain that nurtured the vine. Then the bud that appeared on the vine, and the grape that grew from the bud. *Imagine* that.

Imagine the harvest. What was that like? Who harvested the grapes? What were they wearing? (The people, not the grapes!) Were the grapes picked by hand or machine? How did the grapes turn into raisins?

Imagine tons and tons of grapes that ripen on the vine, then are laid out to dry on heavy brown paper that someone carefully placed on the ground between the grapevines. Did the raisin in your hand dry under the hot southern California sun, or in the furnace at a factory? Imagine the people who placed the brown paper on the ground, who picked all those grapes from the vines and carefully laid them down. What was the weather like? Was it hot? Was it sunny? Did it rain? And imagine the people who checked on the grapes every now and then to see if they were ready. Were they the same people who gathered them up once they were raisins and put them in boxes.

Did you ever look at your food this way before? Do you *think* differently about the raisin in your hand now? Do you *feel* differently about it?

Now it's time to eat. Look at the raisin in front of you again. Pick it up gently between two fingers. Feel the roughness of the surface of the raisin against your skin. Run the tip of your forefinger gently against its wrinkled surface. Try it again with your eyes closed. Can you pick out the individual ridges? The spaces between the ridges? Open up your eyes and cup the raisin in the palm of one hand, then cover it with the palm of your other hand. Now lift your cupped hands to your ear. Shake your hands gently so that the raisin is tossed back and forth like a maraca. If the room is very quiet, you may hear the barely perceptible sound the raisin makes as it bounces around in your hands. Did you ever think you'd listen to a raisin?

Try taking the raisin between your thumb and forefinger and hold it beneath your nose. Let's breathe in. Do you like the smell? It's subtle but sweet. Is the physical sensation pleasant? Unpleasant? Neutral? Do you have any mental reactions to the physical sensation? Do you want to eat it? Not eat it? Do you care one way or another?

Is there anything else going on while you're inhaling the scent of this little raisin? Is anything happening inside your mouth? Many people start salivating long before they pop the raisin in their mouths. Can you feel and hear your stomach growling? Are any emotional reactions showing up to this sensory experience? Do you like raisins? Hate them? Not care?

All right, now it's time to put the raisin in your mouth and to see if you can continue paying attention to all five senses while it's inside your mouth. But don't bite into it yet! Open your mouth and place the raisin on your tongue. Allow your tongue to roll over the irregular texture. Now picture it in your mouth—the dark, nubby skin of the raisin against your sensitive tongue. Can you begin to taste it? The surface of a raisin is sugary sweet, a natural sweetness that comes from the richness of the soil, the sun, and the dehydration that creates this tiny, candylike fruit. Allow yourself time to savor the sweet taste, to feel the raisin's unbroken skin. Maybe you're salivating a little more now in anticipation of what comes next. (Maybe you're salivating just reading about it. The mind is a powerful thing.)

Why don't you suck on the raisin for a moment? When you're sucking, what happens to your throat?

Now bite into it.

Can you hear anything? Can you feel the juice squirt into your cheek? Allow the moistness of your mouth to mix with the juice of the raisin, creating a burst of natural sweetness. How does this feel? Satisfying? Pleasant? Unpleasant? Neutral? Savor the taste as it fills your mouth and sends comforting messages to your brain, letting it know that you're eating and all is well.

Check in with your mind and body once more. Was this fun and would you like to eat another? Or are you bored and would you like to do something else? Don't care one way or the other? What three reactions are these (hint: desire, aversion, indifference)? Have you felt like this after other everyday activities before?

Last, take this opportunity to feel gratitude. Take in the incredible connections between all of the people, places, and things that brought us
these raisins that were once grapes.

Try this a couple of times. You'll never eat a bowl of cereal with raisins
the same way again.

We know from research on adults that mindful eating has health
benefits.[1] However, whether those benefits extend to children is still
an open question because similar research on kids has not yet been
conducted. But it has begun. I am involved in a study conducted
by Drs. Michele Mietus-Snyder of the University of California San
Francisco, Jean Kristeller of Indiana State University, and their colleagues looking into clinical interventions that mitigate the psycho-
social stress and insulin resistance that plagues many overweight
inner-city children. Mietus-Snyder and Kristeller's study targets
preadolescent children who are referred to inner-city weight management clinics. Those who are interested in a lifestyle counseling
program for weight reduction are randomized and enrolled in one
of two intensive eight-week guardian-child group programs: super-
vised exercise or mindfulness-based training. The study looked at
forty obese children and their caregivers. Twenty children and their
caregivers took a weekly exercise class, and the remaining twenty
children and their caregivers took a weekly mindfulness-based
course. They met once a week over a period of eight weeks, and
each class lasted two and a half hours. Both the exercise and mindfulness classes included educational information about healthy
lifestyles and weight loss. At the end of eight weeks, both groups
(exercise and mindfulness) showed improvement over the general
population of similarly situated kids. Participants showed improved
weight loss and reported that their moods and self-concept improved. Strikingly, these benefits remained when the kids were reevaluated two months after the program was completed, and again
when they were reevaluated twelve months after the program was
completed. Both groups—those who took an exercise class and
those who took a mindfulness class—showed significant improvement.[2] These results should not be surprising given that the benefits

of mindful eating in a similar adult population have already been well established.

Your Sense Doors

Once children have learned to pay attention in a refined and friendly way, they're ready to use these new skills to help better understand their inner and outer worlds. Using breath awareness to calm their bodies and concentrate their minds, they're well able to shine a light on the information coming in from the outside world through their sensory systems: the five well-known senses of taste, smell, touch, sight, and hearing, as well as the vestibular system and the proprioceptive systems discussed in Chapter 3. These sensory systems are sometimes called our sense doors.

Noticing what comes in through the sense doors is the first step in developing sensory awareness. The next step is to see how your mind and body respond. Maybe there are automatic ways you respond to relatively innocuous sensory events that you haven't noticed before. You'll find out by noticing your sensory experience from the perspective of a friendly observer. This can be a confusing perspective for kids and parents if they equate observing an experience with being detached from the experience. But that's not how it works, or how it feels. Remember the comparison between the friendly observer and the audience member in Chapter 4 on friendly attention? Here's a similar one I use when talking to parents whose children are musicians: when I meditate and observe my sensory experience, it feels much like the way I feel watching my kids perform in a concert or recital.

Allegra and Gabe have always been interested in music, and as a result I have attended countless concerts and recitals in which they've performed. It is not uncommon for me to feel nervous on their behalf when I watch them perform, even though I am not the one onstage. I know other parents have felt this way, too. Over the past two decades, I've watched my children, my nephews, and their friends perform many times, but not once did I feel like an outside observer. Listening to my kids play, at times I've been overwhelmed by joy and at other times less so because I've heard the song many times before. Here's the part that helps me understand sensory awareness practice: I was completely connected to the experience and always felt something, yet I never lost the perspective of a friendly observer. I knew that they were the performers and I was in the audience, so no matter what I was feeling and how beautiful the song, I never sang along. I participated in their recitals by appreciating their performances, not by performing myself. This is similar to how I notice and experience physical sensations during mindful awareness practice. I may have emotional reactions to what I sense, but I try not to get so caught up in the physical and mental sensations that I identify with them and lose my perspective. It's not uncommon for people to be confused by the stance of the friendly observer and think they must detach themselves from life experience in order to see it clearly. But that is not the case.

What You Hear

My mother had the hearing of a bat. As a child I thought she had superpowers. From her bedroom, she could hear the front doorknob turn when I sneaked into the house late at night. She could hear the freezer door open in the kitchen as I grabbed some ice cream over the din of the TV in the next room. When my friends visited, she could hear and decode our whispers in the bedroom from the backyard as she chatted with my aunt Mary. My mother would have been an exceptional spy.

Lots of moms have this superpower because parents become more attuned to sound by necessity. Parents tune into not just the sound (i.e., voices), but also the origin (coming from the bedroom) plus the tone and feeling (there'll be tears before you know it). We can learn a lot from the feeling and tone of a sound. Let's consider three water sounds: water lapping against moss-covered rocks on the side of a pond; waves crashing against cliffs off the coast of Maine; and the *drip, drip, drip* of water from a leaky faucet. Each water sound evokes entirely different feelings. I often find the sound of water lapping in a pond soothing, but not always. The roar of the ocean is one of my favorite sounds, but it frightens me sometimes. The sound of a leaky faucet annoys me, but it doesn't bother my kids at all. By thinking about what sounds like these stir in your body and mind, you can build awareness of the connections between sensual experiences, your reaction to them, and how those reactions manifest. Here's a worksheet that helps kids make these connections.

Sound of Water	Feeling Category Pleasant, Unpleasant, Neutral	Reactive Category Desire, Aversion, Indifference	Where and How it Shows Up in Mind and Body
Water on rocks	Pleasant	Desire	Body relaxed, breath deepens, mind quiets, content
Ocean waves	Pleasant	Desire	Mind alert, body neutral, happy, excited
Leaky faucet	Unpleasant	Aversion	Mind dull, tired, head aches, feeling overwhelmed

Now let's play some games that will help kids get attuned to their senses from the stance of a friendly and impartial spectator.

SOUND IN SPACE GAME

Here's a variation of the sound awareness practice I described earlier in Chapter 4 in which children listen to the sound of a tone as it fades into the distance. When children no longer hear the sound, they raise their hands. In this variation I make sure that each child has a worksheet and a pencil or pen. I use three different worksheets and three different musical instruments in this game. The number of instruments I use depends on the ages of the children, and the worksheet reflects the number of instruments. There are several variations on this practice. With very young children I only use one instrument, maybe the tone bar. I ring it several times and ask them to count the number of times they hear it ring. If the children are older, I add more instruments, often a drum and jingle bells. You can use any instruments you have handy.

With hands on bellies to feel the movement of the breath in the body, I lead them through the following sequence: "Breathe with hands on belly, look at your focus rocks, and listen for the sounds." I ask the children playing the game to pay careful attention to how many times they hear each sound. After each round, children mark on their worksheets how often they heard each sound.

This game can last quite a while. Remember that there are no right or wrong answers in this game; the question is simply how many times children *heard* the bell, not how many times it was *actually rung*. The answers are not always the same and can provide you with an opportunity to talk to your children about why they may not have heard the bell every time. Did their minds wander? Where was their attention? Where's their attention now?

In Class Worksheet
(version 1)

How many times did you hear the tone bar ring?

#	Tone bar
1	
2	
3	
4	
5	

In Class Worksheet
(version 2)

How many times did you hear the tone bar ring?
How many times did you hear the drum?

#	Tone bar	Drum
1		
2		
3		
4		
5		

In Class Worksheet
(version 3)

How many times did you hear the tone bar ring?
How many times did you hear the drum?
How many times did you hear the bell?

#	Tone bar	Drum	Bell
1			
2			

(continued)

#	Tone bar	Drum	Bell
3			
4			
5			

We play other games to promote mindfulness of sound, too. One of my favorites is listening to what naturally occurs in the environment, as it happens, wherever and whatever that might be. Whether you're in a noisy cafeteria, in your backyard, or in a coffee shop, you can take in the sounds around you like you're listening to music. Scan the sounds you hear and choose one that engages you. Rather than think about what you're hearing, notice the feelings it evokes in your mind and body, relax, and rest in them until the sound fades away, or another sound becomes predominant. If another sound becomes predominant and draws your attention away from the first, that's okay, just notice what happens in your mind and body without getting caught up in it, without analyzing it. Just relax and rest in the experience.

I recently played a variation of this game on the beach with my friend Jenifer, who will be going into kindergarten this year. Jenifer rang the tone bar and listened, but rather than having her raise her hand when the tone faded away, I asked her to raise her hand when the sound of the ocean waves became louder than the sound of the tone. I sat on the beach with her mom Stella and some of our friends as we felt our breathing and listened for Jenifer to ring the tone bar; then we waited to hear the tone fade and the sound of the waves swell. Smiling, Jenifer asked to play again, so we did. But this time at the end of the round, when the sound of the tone had faded away, we sat for a while longer, listening to the sound of the waves break against the beach and feeling the salty breeze against our cheeks.

Jenifer is a little young to fill out a worksheet after playing this game, but when playing with older children, I ask them to make lists of what they heard. If they're playing with friends, they compare lists afterward, and I emphasize that no one's keeping score. It's not a race to hear more sounds. If any of the sounds trigger an emotional reaction, sometimes I use worksheets to help kids connect what they heard with what feelings were triggered and their reaction to these feelings. I also ask kids to tell me where and how the reaction showed up in their minds and bodies. This is how the worksheet of a teenager who spent time listening to sounds in a school cafeteria might look.

Sound	Feeling Category Pleasant, Unpleasant, Neutral	Reactive Category Desire, Aversion, Indifference	Where and How it Shows Up in Mind and Body
Talking	Neutral	Indifference	Didn't notice anything one way or the other
Siren	Unpleasant	Aversion	Alert, felt jumpy, nervous, wanted it to stop
Playground noise	Pleasant	Attraction	Alert, felt a little antsy, wanted to go out and play, too, felt annoyed that I couldn't go out and play

What You Touch

Have you ever visited a haunted house that had a black box with a hole on top large enough to put your hand through but small enough to obscure what was inside? Usually those boxes are filled with slippery wet noodles, peeled grapes, cushiony cotton batons, and other sensory-rich objects that are terrific for building awareness of touch and of our reaction to how something feels. Try it with your children using one of the worksheets, and see what happens when they touch something gooey, for example: Is the sensation pleasant, unpleasant, or neutral? What do their minds want you to do when they touch it? If they're touching something gooey, do they want to pull away or mush around in it? What if they reach in and find something cool, oblong, and smooth, about the size of their palm: Is the sensation pleasant, unpleasant, or neutral? Do they hold it in their hand? Do they quickly drop it? Does it remind them of anything? Here's a worksheet to give them if you'd like to give this game a try.

Description of How the Object Feels	Did It Feel... Nice? Not Nice? Neither one nor the other?	What Did You Want to Do? Keep touching it? Stop touching it?	See If You Can Guess What It Was

There is another sensory awareness game that's a fun and a brilliant way to help children increase awareness of mental and physical sensations, their reactions to them, and what happens if they *do not* react, even if they have the impulse to react. I learned it in my first childbirth class.

MELTING-ICE GAME

All the children have a cube of ice in a cup and a napkin. They hold the ice cube in the palm of their hands for as long as possible, even though it burns a little. If holding the ice cube becomes too uncomfortable before it melts, they can slide it back into the cup and retrieve it when they're ready. While holding the ice, the children name the sensations they're experiencing—burning, cold, stinging—and mentally place them in one of three categories—pleasant, unpleasant, or neutral. At first, the category is almost always unpleasant, but not too hard to deal with. Soon, though, most kids feel "freezer burn," and the stinging becomes harder and harder to tolerate. Then the sensation tends to change. It can be difficult but, if the children hang on for a while, their palms begin to numb, and the stinging becomes less intense. The burning eases, and other sensory experiences show up as cold-water puddles in their palms or drips onto their legs. Throughout this process, feelings and reactions are usually triggered in the children's bodies and minds. All the experiences—emotions, thoughts, and physical sensations—are fodder for later discussion about the distinction between sense impressions, physical reactions, and mental reactions.

The second time we play the game, the emphasis is on what it takes *not to react* to the ice, both mentally and physically. The mind affects the body and vice versa, and mental and physical states are not always aligned, but both mental and physical states are always changing. After this round of the game, older children and teens fill out worksheets to distinguish between direct, sensual experiences and those we filter through emotions, thoughts, and mental associations. Here's a worksheet showing how three different teenagers might view exactly the same experience.

Direct Sensory Experience	Category	Physical Reaction	Emotional Reaction	Associations
Freezer burn	Unpleasant	Keep on holding the ice	Fear and shame	That was so hard for me, and it's easy for everyone else. I'm such a loser.

(continued)

Direct Sensory Experience	Category	Physical Reaction	Emotional Reaction	Associations
Freezer burn	Unpleasant	Keep on holding the ice	Accomplishment	If I put my mind to something, I can do it, even though it's difficult.
Freezer burn	Unpleasant	Keep on holding the ice	Pride	Look at me! I am so much tougher than these other kids. I can't believe they couldn't even hold an ice cube for a few minutes.

Even though I don't insist that kids close their eyes if they don't want to, some sensory-awareness games are more fun when they do. Often having children close their eyes during games is less problematic than having them close their eyes during meditation, especially when the games involve sitting up rather than lying down. Kids generally feel comfortable closing their eyes for this game, and it's a favorite of my elementary school students. Some even like to play wearing a blindfold.

WHAT'S BEHIND MY BACK?

The kids close their eyes and put their hands behind their backs while you place small objects (erasers, stones, tiny rubber ducks or dinosaurs, dice, slippery things, rough things) in each of their hands. Now ask them to describe how their object feels, what they think it looks like, whether it's hard or soft, what its shape is. After each person describes his or her object, see if anyone else can guess what it is, and then have that child show the object to the group. Go around the circle till all the kids have had a chance to describe what they're holding. It's fun for them to describe things, hear each other's descriptions, and what they guess.

What You See

Many common childhood games, like memory games and puzzles, promote mindfulness of what you see and are excellent attention-building activities. Here are a few to practice at home.

KIM'S GAME
Take a number of everyday household objects (a rubber ball, playing cards, jacks, a seashell, a stone, etc.), place them on a tray, and cover them with a cloth. Give everybody a piece of paper and a pencil, then explain: There are [however many] common objects on this tray that I'm covering with a blanket. Remind the children not to look until they're all covered up! Now pick up the blanket for ten seconds. 1-2-3-4-5-6-7-8-9-10. Then, quickly cover everything back up and see how many covered objects the children remember. Ask the children to open their eyes and write down the names of the objects they thought they saw, then uncover the objects so they can check their lists against what is actually there.

The next game brings out the architect and interior designer in all of us. Ask your children to draw a picture of everything they remember from one particular place. It could be a bedroom, a desk, a bookshelf, the backyard . . . anywhere at all.

DRAW A PICTURE OF YOUR ROOM
Grab a piece of paper right now and draw your bedroom from memory. (No peeking!) Well done! Now go into your bedroom, take a look around, and fill in the blanks. Pay attention to what you drew from memory and what you added later. It's surprising how many details we don't take in, or forget about, even in very familiar places.

Awareness of Your Body as a Whole

The preceding sensory awareness activities range from mindful eating, in which children pay attention to information coming in through all the sense doors at once, to games like Sound in Space, in which children carefully focus on a single sense impression. This next practice is intended to heighten awareness of the whole body. It's a visualization about all the special stars in the sky, one for each person on the planet. It can be practiced either sitting up or lying down, and it starts with the children paying attention to the feeling of their breath as it moves in and out of their bodies. Once they are resting in the gentle rising and falling of breath, I begin to talk about imaginary stars in the sky.

SPECIAL STAR

Everyone has his or her own special star, a star that is with you all of the time. Like a shadow, your special star stays with you when you're eating, sleeping, playing, and having fun. But unlike your shadow, your star brings light, not shade. Your special star follows you to school, to karate or soccer practice, to a play date at your friend's house, and then back home again. This special star is all your own.

What does it look like? It can be just as you want it to be. It can be any shape, any size, any color; it can be made out of silk, out of fur, out of cotton balls—anything at all. See if you can imagine a star that brings a smile to your face when you think about it. Maybe it's shiny, maybe it's soft, maybe it's polka-dotted. Whatever your star looks like and feels like, it's yours alone.

Like everything else, your star can change. Maybe it's large some days, small others, hot and then cool. That's up to you. But whatever your star looks and feels like, it's comforting to know that it is always there.

Now imagine that your star is in the sky right now, and you can feel its warm light on your body. Imagine what your skin feels like when it's bathed in the warmth of your own special star. Feel the warmth on the top of your head, your forehead, over your ears, your cheeks, your nose, your whole face, your chin, even your neck. Now slowly let the feeling of warm light move down over your shoulders and expand to include your chest and torso, your arms, your hands, and your fingers. Now the warmth is moving into your middle and lower body, warming up your upper legs, knees, lower legs, feet, and toes.

Wow. It feels just great to rest and be me.

Now, one last time, let's imagine that we can see our stars and feel their warmth cover our whole bodies like cozy blankets. Imagine, really imagine, what that looks and feels like. Now imagine the warmth from your star is like a blanket softly falling against your skin; it relaxes your whole body so you can rest.

Making Music Together and Leading a Mindfulness Band

Kids of all ages are natural percussionists, and they love to drum with whatever makeshift instruments they can get their hands on. Toddlers naturally pound away on the tray tables of their high chairs, and teenagers often use knives and forks to tap out a rhythm at the dinner table. Pots, pans, and wooden salad bowls are all tools for your child's creativity. With a bit of ingenuity you can transform your kitchen cupboards into a treasure trove of makeshift instruments, and watch your kids blossom into drummers who rival Stewart Copeland of the Police and Ringo Starr of the Beatles. Just play some songs that you enjoy and drum along with them, or you can drum together without any music in the background at all. Following one another's rhythm, tuning in to one another, and to the music are all activities that promote mindful listening.

If you're the leader of this mindfulness band, keep in mind that these impromptu jam sessions can get chaotic quickly. To stay on track:

• Keep a beat going.

• Keep structure to the activity.

- Include equal parts of both silence and drumming.

- End the song if the activity begins to feel, and sound, more frenetic than patterned and you can't rein it in.

When you have finished drumming together, and the laughter has subsided, sit quietly and rest in the relative sound of silence and the rising and falling of your breathing. As a parent or teacher you don't have to say the words *mindfulness* or *meditation* even once, but still, if you follow these simple guidelines, by the end of this activity there's often a feeling of mindful attunement in the room, attunement with one another and with the music. It can feel as if mindfulness happened all by itself.

Sensory awareness practices can be fun without taking much time or many materials. There's usually something in your kitchen cupboard that's rich with sensory information: kidney beans, lentils, black beans, walnuts, peanuts, cotton balls, shaving cream, frozen peas, and slivered almonds are all great objects to use in these games.

SORTING BEANS WITH YOUR EYES CLOSED

The next time you're stuck indoors on a rainy afternoon, open the kitchen cupboard and pull out a few bags of beans. A handful of red kidney beans, black beans, and lentils will do the trick. If you have a bag of peas in the freezer, you can use them, too. Place a few of each variety in a bowl, cover the bowl with a napkin, and put it on the table along with four empty glasses or teacups. Now you are ready to play the game. Usually we sort things by how they look, but in this game we will sort things by how they feel.

Ask your children to close their eyes, or tie scarves around their heads as blindfolds. Once their eyes are covered, take the cloth off the bowl and place it in front of them. Now, help them pick the beans or frozen peas out one by one. Together roll them between your fingers, compare them by describing how they feel, and place the beans or peas into one of several cups by category (you'll have one cup for each type—for example, big beans, little beans, oblong beans, and cold peas). Because the children are blindfolded, you'll probably want them to tell you what type of bean it is so that you can put the beans in the appropriate cup for them. For example, the cold round ones go into one cup (they're the frozen peas). The oblong, hard ones go into another cup (they're the kidney beans). The tiny beans are lentils, and they go in a third cup. After all the beans have been sorted, ask your children what type of bean they think is in each cup. Now take off the blindfolds and check it out. Together you can talk about how much we rely on our sense of sight. But how, when we take away our sight, we can also learn a lot about things through our other senses.

Tools to Raise Awareness

Kids can tell what's happening in their inner and outer worlds by paying close attention to the information that comes in through their sense doors. The mind meter gives them a fun way to tell us what is happening in their minds and bodies, without their having to put what they notice into words.

You can make a photocopy of this "Mind Meter" and color the triangles three different colors for the Mind Meter Game, in which children answer questions by pointing toward the triangle that best describes how they're feeling. The point of the game is to help children make observations and describe their present-moment experience. Because kids are simply describing how they feel, there are no right or wrong answers, so long as they are respectful to other people and themselves. When working with young children, my first question is usually whether it's easy or hard for them to sit still right now. Here's how I do it:

> *I'm going to ask a question and have you point to the colored triangle on the Mind Meter that best describes how you feel right now. Make sure to wait until I say, "Go!" The question is whether it's easy or hard to sit still right now. If you're having a hard time sitting still, point to the red triangle; if it's easy, point to the blue; if it's not hard, not easy, but something in between, point to the yellow. "Ready, Set, Go!"*

Kids can easily get distracted. It's not uncommon for them to look to see where their friends are pointing before pointing themselves, just to make sure they're playing the game correctly. Saying "Ready, set, go!" or "One, two, three, point!" to start the game helps avoid this problem. This game builds kids' awareness of what their bodies are telling them with signals like stiffness, fatigue, soreness, and hunger. It also gives me an opportunity to encourage kids to listen to what their bodies have to say.

The Mind Meter has several other quite practical applications, not the least of which is that it gives me an idea of how the children I'm working with feel. With a quick Mind Meter question I can get a sense of whether they're having trouble sitting still. (And, if they are, it's time to play a game that's more physically active.) By encouraging kids to check one another's Mind Meters after everyone has pointed to a triangle, kids can recognize that their impressions are not unique. They are not alone when they feel physically uncomfortable, bored, or silly.

I use the Mind Meter to promote awareness of both mind and body states, and I choose my questions based on the quality I hope to encourage, or the experience I hope the child will better understand. For instance, if I think a child is cranky because she's hungry, I would ask, "Does your stomach feel full, empty, or comfortable?" Here are some questions I've asked to promote specific qualities that mindful awareness develops.

To Build Awareness Of . . .	Ask . . .
Attention	*Are you focused, concentrated, distracted, or in between?*
Attention	*Is it easy to pay attention, hard to pay attention, or in between?*
Clarity	*Do you feel confused, clear, or in between?*
Clarity	*Is doing this (it could be anything—sitting still, working on math homework) easy, hard, or in between?*
Patience	*Do you feel patient, impatient, or in between?*
Friendliness	*Do you feel friendly, unfriendly, or in between?*
Interconnectedness	*Do you feel on your own, part of a community, or in between?*
Adaptability	*Do you feel interested, uninterested, or in between?*
Wakefulness	*Do you feel sluggish, energetic, or in between?*
Physical ease or relaxation	*Is it easy to sit still, hard to sit still, or in between?*
Relaxation	*Do you feel tense, relaxed, or in between?*

Mindfulness Together:
Thumbs-Up, Thumbs-Down,
or Thumbs-Sideways

You don't need Mind Meter cards to play the Mind Meter Game at home with your kids or in a classroom. The same questions can also be answered using hand signals—with a thumbs-up, a thumbs-down, or a thumbs-sideways. Like the Mind Meter, hand signals can help children develop awareness of what is happening in their minds and bodies and to communicate it nonverbally. For example, if the question is whether it's easy or hard to sit still, rather than responding to questions by pointing to the colored triangle that best describes how they're feeling, they give a thumbs-up if it's easy to sit still, a thumbs-down if it's hard, and a thumbs-sideways if it's in between.

There's a Whole Lot of Confusion About Now

Another objective of the Mind Meter Game is to help children better understand their present moment experience, specifically what's happening in their minds and bodies right now. I use the Hello Game for this purpose, too.

HELLO GAME—WHAT'S COMING IN THROUGH YOUR SENSES NOW?

In this version of the Hello Game, we go around the circle (or dinner table), turning to our neighbor, making eye contact, and saying hello. When emphasizing awareness of our bodies, use a greeting that highlights sense impressions, like identifying one bodily sensation without labeling it good or bad. For example, "Hello, my shoulder feels stiff," or "Hello, my feet are cold."

Or you can ask a child to say "Hello" and then identify an impression that's coming through one of his or her senses, like, "Hello, my socks are soft," or "Hello, I see a globe in the corner of the room," or "Hello, I smell the cookies baking in the oven," or "Hello, I taste the mint flavor of my gum," or "Hello, I hear the furnace roaring in the next room."

Like the Mind Meter Game, the point of this prompt is to identify a present-moment sense impression and to describe it. As we take turns saying "Hello," children frequently analyse their experience without realizing it, like saying, "Hello, that poster on the wall is cool." These comments are a great opportunity to point out how opinions that we may not even realize we have can sneak into what we say and do, and you can suggest that the child describe the poster again in neutral language. He or she might rephrase the description to "I see a rock 'n' roll poster on the wall."

This may seem like a minor point, but I find that these exercises are useful in helping kids learn to objectively observe and describe present moment experience before drawing any conclusions. It's an opportunity to remind children that developing sound judgment is important and related to clear seeing. In order for a children or teenagers to see clearly, they must be aware of their own opinions and distinguish between them and descriptions.

Some assume that focusing on the present moment means ignoring the past and the future, but that's not the way it works. Everything that leads up to this very moment is part of now. Our goals, expectations, and fears about the future are also part of now. I could no more dislodge my childhood from myself than I could dislodge my bones from my body. My past experience influences what I'm doing right now. What I hope will (or will not) happen in the future also influences what I'm doing and typing now.

Don't get me wrong, I'm not thinking about the past or the future as I type. Nor will I think about the past or future when I meditate later. But that doesn't mean past experience and future expectations are not influencing my present-moment experience. I don't need to be thinking about something for it to inform my perspective.

Most children and teens understand intuitively that the past, present, and future are naturally interwoven. Middle and high school kids in particular tend to have a clear sense that what they're doing now will have an effect on what will happen next—both present action and future expectations relate to what they've said or done before. Teenagers don't need to think about this sequence much; they tend to know it already because, by the time they're in high school, most have learned the hard way that actions have consequences. They understand that if there is a test coming up (in the future), it is important to study (now), and they know how to study (now) because they have studied for many, many other tests throughout their school career (in the past). In other words, if they don't study their notes from yesterday's class right now, they are likely to bomb tomorrow's exam.

A misunderstanding of the concept of now can be a slippery slope that quickly leads to a feeling of hopelessness. If kids view what's happening in the present moment as separate from past and future experience, figuring that what they say or do makes little difference is an understandable conclusion. Understandable, but at odds with two basic foundations of mindfulness practice: that all actions have consequences and that everything changes. In a worldview that is informed by a visceral understanding of interdependence and impermanence absolutely . . . every . . . moment . . . matters.

Mindfulness Together:
Listening to What Our Bodies
Are Trying to Tell Us

The nature of everyone's mind is clear and sensitive to each experience that arises in and around us. But that fundamental clarity and sensitivity can be hidden by thoughts, emotions, and projections. Imagine yourself, on a warm summer night, looking up at an indigo sky with glittering stars, moons, and planets as far as the eye can see. Now imagine looking up on a cloudy night. The planets and stars are still in the sky, but you can't see them anymore. The vast, tranquil sky is always inside of us. Meditation can peel away the layers of mental bric-a-brac that cloud the natural clarity of our minds.

Sitting on a cushion cross-legged for an extended period of time is one of many ways to meditate. But there are other less formal ways to meditate as well. Meaningful insights can be found in a flash of understanding while doing routine chores around the house. The key to practicing meditation in the midst of daily life is to rest in what's happening at the time, as it's happening, without overthinking it. This usually takes a shift in perspective.

To effectively organize and navigate car pools, doctors' appointments, meetings, homework, after-school schedules, and the myriad other activities that make up family life, parents often adopt a mind-set like that of tactical military commanders who are fixated on logistics—the polar opposite of the open, sensitive mind-set of meditation. Shifting gears from a logistical frame of mind to a non-conceptual one is a lot to ask of anyone and, for those who are new to meditation, can lead to disappointment. There are, however, many ways to bridge these two poles and make it easier to transition. The last thing I want is for parents to feel they failed at meditation because their minds are not always peaceful when they meditate. So I encourage them to listen to music, sip a cup of tea, take a hot bath, or walk in the garden before settling down to meditate. Here's a suggestion for you to try at home.

Before you begin, I encourage you to check on the time. It doesn't matter how much time you have: if you have five minutes, a half hour, or more, that's enough for you to practice mindfulness. If there's something you need to do at a certain time, it's a good idea to set a timer. I use my cell phone and set my ringtone to the sound of crickets chirping.

Brew a cup of hot tea before you meditate. While waiting for the water to boil, I suggest you sit in a comfortable chair and relax. Try not to think about logistics right now; instead, use the time to do something pleasant like listen to music or leaf through a book, magazine, or photo album. Whatever you do, *do not* spend this time doing chores. Right now, please take these few minutes for yourself and rest. If thoughts come to mind about things you have to do, or should be doing, please notice them and put them aside. You can think about them later; right now the aim is to shift gears away from thinking and analyzing life and toward feeling and experiencing it.

Once the kettle is ready and you've made your tea, sit quietly and cradle the cup in your hands. How does the warmth of the ceramic feel against your palms? Breathe deeply and relax. See if you can drink your tea slowly and deliberately and notice the thoughts, emotions, and physical sensations that come to mind as you sip.

An enormous amount of information about the outside world is available to us all of the time when we pay attention to what's coming in through our sense doors. As you drink your tea, reflect on what your body might be trying to tell you. Do you feel any tension or kinks in your body? Does taking time to relax change how your body feels? Does it feel pleasant, unpleasant, or neutral? Have any qualities in your body or mind shifted by taking time out of your day to mindfully enjoy a cup of tea?

See if you can drink your tea without looking at your timer. If it rings, before you have a chance to meditate, congratulations! Mindfully sipping your cup of tea is a form of meditation itself. From the perspective of mindfulness, bringing awareness to the sensations in your mind and body as you drink your tea, as they are happening and without needing to name them, is a sensory awareness practice. Slowing down to drink tea mindfully helps build our capacity to notice the information about the outside world coming into our minds through the sense doors of our bodies.

If you still have some time, let's close this mindfulness practice with simple breath and body awareness. For this, you'll put your tea down and sit comfortably wherever you are, with your hands on your knees, feet flat on the floor, back straight, chin tucked, and eyes gazing downward softly, or closed, whichever is most comfortable for you. Scan your body with your attention briefly, and if you feel any discomfort or tension, you can shift your physical posture so that you are more comfortable. If it's not possible for you to sit upright comfortably now, you might want to lie flat on your back on the floor with eyes closed or gazing down toward your chest.

Whatever posture you choose—sitting or lying down—once you're physically comfortable, simply settle into the feeling of the movement of your breath through your body.

I encourage you to take whatever time you have left to rest mindfully. Breathe in and relax. Breathe out and release any tension in your mind and body. See if you can keep your mind on the feeling of the movement of your breath through your body. Breathe in, breathe out, notice these simple acts that are the foundation of our lives.

Mindfulness Together

Now that you've practiced sensory awareness yourself by mindfully holding and sipping your cup of tea, you can practice something similar with your children. For example, you can mindfully sip hot chocolate together. You might ask whether they like the way the warm cup feels against their palms. Describe how the cup feels against your palms. If there's steam coming up from the milk, you might lean over to see if you can feel it against your nose, cheeks, or forehead and encourage your children to do the same. If drinking hot chocolate together in this way makes you feel relaxed and happy, you might mention that, too. If you like, you can talk about mindfulness, but there is no need to mention it at all. It doesn't matter what name you place on what you're doing. Regardless of what you call it, kindly helping your children become more aware of information from the outside world coming in through their sense doors, and taking a moment to experience it, is practicing mindfulness together.

Chapter 7

Emotional Freedom:

Release Yourself from

Destructive Thoughts

and Feelings

I wish I had no problems
I wish I was in middle school
I wish I had a sister
I wish I had all the wishes I want.

Sixth-grade student

When Gabe was ten and Allegra was twelve, I thought that taking them to witness a Buddhist life release ceremony could be a meaningful family outing. The goal really wasn't to instill Buddhist beliefs and customs in the kids. It was a beautiful winter day, and I'd never attended a life release ceremony myself—even though I had read about them—and Seth and I were curious. So we all climbed in the car and drove to Marina del Rey.

This monthly fish release ceremony held for the liberation of all beings was sponsored by the Karma Kagyu Study Group in Los Angeles, an organization that was affiliated with a Tibetan lama who lived in New York. Participants met at the sportfishing bait shop and purchased, at half price, live baitfish for use in the ceremony. About thirty-five participants bought thousands of sardines and anchovies that would ordinarily have been used by fisherman as bait. We plunked down $20 for a tin bucket of water filled with swimming fish and a ladle. Our donation was (pardon the pun) a drop in the bucket compared to the others who bought barrels of fish from the bemused shopkeeper for over $1,000.

We waited on the dock for the arrival of the lamas, who would conduct the ceremony and chant the prayers. The setting was beautiful, the kids were excited, and we were touched by the warm community of all shapes, sizes, ages, and colors gathered that afternoon to celebrate life and freedom. Freedom is a fundamental value of the Judeo-Christian traditions in which we were raised, and it seemed right for our family to join in their extension to the Buddhist life release ceremony. As we ruminated on these concepts in the glow of family and new friends, Seth and I noticed two fishermen on the edge of the dock, hooks baited, ready and waiting. We didn't mention anything to the kids, but he and I realized that they were lurking on the fringe of the ceremony to catch the larger fish—halibut, sea bass and barracuda—that would swarm toward the dock once the baitfish had been released.

Soon five monks in saffron robes and sandals arrived and began the ceremony by singing, "*Om Mani Peme Hung*," a Tibetan chant of compassion. Allegra, Seth, Gabe, and I took turns ladling the baitfish out of the metal bucket and releasing them into the harbor. Other participants, those who had purchased hundreds of dollars' worth of fish, were scooping their fish out of a large bait pool behind the dock. Thousands and thousands of fish were released that morning in the spirit of freedom.

By now, Gabe and Allegra, too, had noticed the fishermen at the end of the dock, baiting up their hooks for the larger fish swimming in from the ocean to gobble up the smaller ones we had set free. I still hoped they'd see the ceremony as we did, as a way to deepen our appreciation for life and freedom. And even if a couple of fishermen used the bait fish we'd released to catch their lunch, the touch of irony wouldn't spoil the symbolism. As parents we expose our kids to cultural experiences in the hope that those experiences will expand their horizons and help them see the world in a new way. And sometimes we know immediately that it worked. Other times, however, we're not sure, or we fear that the whole idea landed with a thud.

This was one of those times. Then we heard someone calling, a bearded guy with a pencil and reporter's pad in hand, running up the stairs and asking us to stop for a moment to talk with him. He was a reporter doing a story on the fish release ceremony for the *Los Angeles Times*. He wanted to ask Allegra and Gabe about their impressions of the ceremony. Looking this stranger in the eye with a quizzical expression, Gabe explained, "It just makes you feel good about yourself to set something free." And Allegra chimed in, "It's about getting a second chance. If I get captured, I hope the Buddhists set me free."

Fishermen or no fishermen, the kids had gotten the message.

SETTING THE LADYBUGS FREE

You can have your own life release ceremony with a cardboard box full of ladybugs from a garden store or crickets from the pet store. Gather the kids around and tell the little creatures you hope they'll live in freedom again. Opening the box, set them free and watch them crawl through the grass, going their different ways. You can send them friendly wishes hoping they'll be happy, healthy, safe, and live in peace. It doesn't matter if half of them are eaten by birds within a few minutes. What matters is that you set them free.

Awareness of Thoughts, Emotions, and How We React to Them

Just as we set ladybugs and fish free, we can also set our own minds free with certain mindfulness techniques. In our quest for psychological freedom we call on the friendly observer again, and we bring our awareness to thoughts and emotions and how we react to them. We experience the activity in our minds with interest and engagement but without getting caught up in the stories that often go along with our emotions. This can be difficult, especially if we over-identify with our thoughts and emotions. Dr. Jeffrey Schwartz, in his book *Dear Patrick,* expands on this to a teenage rower whom he mentored in the late 1990s:

> Look at your hand. While you're looking at it, make a fist.
>
> Now would you say, "I'm clenched"? Of course not. It's your hand that's clenched. You're the one who decided to clench it.
>
> Now "look at" your mood—that is, make a mental note of it.
>
> I bet you'll immediately think something like, "I'm happy," or "I'm sad," or "I'm restless," or "bored," or whatever it happens to be right now. But I've got news for you: the very fact that you can observe your mood and describe it—just as you could your hand—means that you are not it. Remember this, because it's the heart of the matter: If you can observe it and describe it, it's not you—not the core you, the real you. . . . [1]

Thoughts and emotions are part of who we are, but they aren't the whole picture. They are a reflection of the dynamic activity that occurs naturally in our minds and they ebb, flow, and eventually wash through us.

As kids get older and develop the attention control necessary to view their thoughts and emotions clearheadedly, they begin to get a sense of what's going on in their minds. With strong, stable attentional skills it becomes possible for them to experience emotions as they unfold and stay steady if painful reactions occur in their wake. The stance of a friendly observer discourages preadolescents and teens from overidentifying with their thoughts and emotions, and it encourages them to view their feelings differently. Instead of thinking, "I am angry," the friendly observer sees that "I have an angry feeling." In *Dear Patrick,* Schwartz characterizes this as understanding the difference between "me and my brain." Making a nuanced distinction between "me and my brain" or "me and my body" can be challenging and requires a level of maturity that some kids haven't yet developed, but is a valuable exercise.

Awareness of Thoughts

Here are some games and activities that encourage older children and teenagers to bring friendly awareness to their thoughts. How to watch your mind, not just during meditation but throughout the day, can be a tricky thing to explain to anyone, but the John Lennon song "Watching the Wheels" does a pretty good job of it. Lennon wrote "Watching the Wheels" about his six-year break from the music industry during the mid to late 1970s. In the lyrics he writes that "people say I'm crazy, dreaming my life away" and explains how he now spends his time watching the wheels go round and round. He elaborates that he no longer rides the merry-go-round and that he had to let it go.

When singing John Lennon's song "Wheels" with kids, I change the last lyric to "I just watch and let it go." I ask them if they've seen a hamster running around on a wheel. Most of them have. Then I ask if it ever feels like they have a hamster wheel in their heads, with thoughts and emotions spinning around in their minds like a hamster on a wheel. Most children say they've felt that way, and that they bet John Lennon felt like that, too. We talk about what Lennon might have meant by: "I love to watch them roll," and how watching the wheels roll is not the same as getting caught up on the merry-go-round of life. This song has been a springboard for many spirited discussions about stress, materialism, the various merry-go-rounds kids are on, and the ways they can get off of them. Students have noticed for themselves that fame and fortune can be enslaving. Leafing through the tabloids at the checkout counter, with their moms, teens see that some basic freedoms that they take for granted—like eating ice cream uninterrupted, or going out to buy a carton of milk in grungy clothes with dirty hair—are not available to celebrities. They empathize with what John Lennon's life must have been like and with the lives of others like him.

MONKEY CHAINS

There is a colorful children's toy called Barrel of Monkeys; it's a plastic barrel filled with toy monkeys that I use when practicing mindfulness with kids. The plastic monkeys' arms are shaped like hooks, so kids can make a monkey chain by hanging them arm by arm. It's a lively, fun way to demonstrate how we relate to thoughts and emotions during introspective practice. Afterward I ask kids what they were distracted by while practicing mindfulness of breathing or Slow and Silent Walking. Kids take turns answering, and every time someone mentions a thought, emotion, or physical sensation, I pull a monkey out of the barrel to represent the distraction and hang it on the chain. Adding monkey after monkey to the chain, I point out that, when practicing mindfulness of breathing, no one monkey (or distraction) is considered more meaningful than another, and that we deal with every distraction in the same way. Regardless of their content, every thought is a distraction and every emotion is another distraction. I ask, "What do we do with distractions when we notice them?" Then comes the children's favorite part: They call out, "Let them go," or "Dump them," and I drop the monkey chain and they clatter back into the barrel before we start all over again.

HELLO GAME—WHAT'S COMING AND GOING IN YOUR MIND RIGHT NOW?

In this version of the Hello Game, we go around the circle (or dinner table), turning to our neighbor, making eye contact, and saying hello. Then we mention one thing we're thinking right now. To reinforce awareness of how often kids are distracted, and how often our minds have wandered into the past or present, I ask kids to place whatever they're thinking about into one of three categories—past, present, or future. For example, you might make eye contact with your daughter and say, "Good morning, I'm thinking about your birthday party right now." In response, she might say, "Hi,

Mom, I'm thinking about my birthday, too, now that you mentioned it." The next step is to identify whether we're thinking about something in the past, present, or future. In this case the birthday party is either in the past or the future. You can repeat the game with awareness of emotions rather than thoughts; in this case the prompt might be to say hello and tell her what you're thinking or feeling right now. With a little ingenuity, there are an infinite number of hello prompts you can come up with that will teach important lessons.

Awareness of Automatic Behavior

Few things limit our psychological, physical, and emotional freedom more than personal habits of speech, thought, and action that we don't know we have. Albert Einstein defined insanity as "doing the same thing over and over again and expecting different results," and for better or worse, we all have habits—some of them helpful or neutral, but others that persistently create problems in our lives. Deeply ingrained habits can lead to a type of insanity in many people, both children and adults, but it's easier for kids to change habits than for grown-ups. One way to start recognizing your patterns is to create external signals that will automatically show up throughout the day. These interrupters provide an opportunity to pause and:

- Reflect on your motivation (Is it friendly or unfriendly?).

- Reflect on whether the actions likely to spring from that motivation will steer you toward happiness (or not).

- Shift gears, if necessary, toward an action or mental state that's more conducive to happiness.

Here are some activities that gently interrupt automatic behavior.

MINDFULNESS BELL

A well-known practice for interrupting everyday life is a mindfulness bell. Vietnamese Zen master Thich Nhat Hanh recommends that families use the mindfulness bell to signal that it's time to take a brief break from whatever they're doing and check their breathing. The bell can be anything that makes a pleasant and sustained sound. The integration of a mindfulness bell into your family routine often yields surprising and fun opportunities for awareness.

- *You can use it to get your children's attention without bellowing above the din of television, radio, music, or other household noise.*

- *When it looks like your children are moving so fast and furiously that they'll soon physically or emotionally crash, you can slow that momentum by ringing the bell.*

- *You might empower your kids to ring the mindfulness bell whenever they would like the entire family to pause and reflect. The first time a child uses the mindfulness bell can come as a surprise to his or her parents. Several parents have described the same scene to me. They are interrupted in the middle of an argument by the ringing of the mindfulness bell and, when they look over to find that their child is the one who is ringing it, the parents burst into laughter. This is one of my all-time-favorite examples of how parents can empower children to take care of themselves. What a great way to resolve conflict and model conflict resolution for kids.*

A STRING AROUND YOUR FINGER

You can also create mindfulness reminders and put them around your house or wear them. I've seen kids tie a string around one finger, make mindfulness bracelets of ribbons or beads, tape a small piece of colorful scotch tape on the inside of their cell phones, and stick a Post-it on their computer screens or refrigerators. These physical reminders are effective ways to integrate friendly awareness into your daily routine. Whenever you see them, just pause to take in what's happening in your mind and body.

BREATHING PROMPTS

Every day kids engage in routine tasks like brushing their teeth or putting on their socks. You can suggest to your children that they choose one of these relatively mundane daily activities and use it as an opportunity to practice breath awareness. For example, they could stop and breathe every evening before they brush their teeth, or in the morning when they put on their shoes and socks. Breathing prompts help kids recognize how many things they do on automatic pilot. By interrupting automatic behavior, kids have the time and mental space to make connections between what they're doing, what they're thinking, and how they're feeling. Even very young children can make these connections. You can ask them:

- *How their breath feels just before going to sleep and just after waking up each day.*
- *How their breath feels when they run and play.*
- *How their breath feels when they ride in a car or bus on their way to school.*
- *How their breath feels when they're laughing or just after they laugh.*

If I had to choose only one activity for kids to practice at home, it would be breathing prompts, because they've facilitated more meaningful shifts in behavior among my students and their families than any other mindfulness practice I teach.

Awareness of Emotions and Emotional Reactivity

Once kids become aware of painful emotions, it's not always easy for them to talk about them. Trudy Goodman, a meditation teacher and psychologist who has worked extensively with children and families, suggests a creative starting point for conversations about emotion based on a classical practice that compares difficult emotions to visitors who come and go. Like house guests, some emotions are welcome, and others are not. Some stop by at a convenient time, and others don't. Even welcome visitors who stop by at a good time can overstay their welcome. When they do, it's helpful to remember that visitors, by definition, will not stay forever. By personifying emotions as visitors, we can playfully talk with children about emotions, even painful ones. As kids watch the energy of emotion unfold, or unravel, they can begin to recognize that emotional pain, like cranky visitors, will leave eventually. I've found this method helpful particularly when working with younger kids.

Sitting in a circle and talking about your feelings in the spirit of kindness and compassion can be revolutionary for children and teenagers. In *The Way of Council*, Jack Zimmerman quoted my colleague Tom Nolan who observed: "Encouraging children to speak from the heart is a strong message. It helps educate them about their emotions by asking how they feel and then giving them an opportunity to wrestle with expressing an answer."[2] It's important for a child's social, emotional, and neurological development to have a safe place where they can speak from their heart without fear of being shamed or judged. Sadly, not all children have one. Dr. Mark Brady, a social neuroscience educator, has written about the negative neurological impact of not being free to speak your truth as a child:

Lying is something I was trained to do well as a kid, by parents, teachers and adults who didn't really want to hear the truth, and who regularly punished anyone who shared it unvarnished. Getting yelled at or punished for truth-telling it turns out can't compete with the relief from stress and tension that lying provides in the moment. I think it would have been better to have been offered an environment where it was safe to tell hard truths, and then also be taught how to manage the adrenaline and cortisol that is often triggered in response by people like Tom Cruise, in the movie *A Few Good Men*, who can't really handle such truths. This would require parents, teachers, and such becoming skilled at managing their own emotional reactivity, of course. How likely is that?[3]

Nolan's and Brady's comments highlight again that it is crucial for anyone who wants to teach children mindfulness to have an established practice themselves and to be skilled at managing their own emotional reactivity and staying steady in the face of kids' emotional reactivity.

When setting the tone for a mindfulness circle, it's important to keep in mind that, as the facilitator, your role is not to give advice or council, but to help the children understand their experience the best they can, from the inside out. This can be a tough role to take when we want nothing more than to fix the situation and stop children from hurting. We also remind our students that it's not their role to give advice either. Everyone—children, teens, and adults—is charged with bringing the same quality of attention, kindness, and witnessing to the mindfulness circle that they bring to meditation practice.

In mindfulness circles I remind everyone that each moment is an opportunity to watch their own minds, even when it's not their turn to speak. Instead of becoming enmeshed in a mental rehearsal of what they plan to say before their turn comes along, or silently rehashing what they said after having spoken, these are opportunities to notice how their minds react to listening to other people's stories and to the telling of their own.

Sitting in a circle, speaking your truth, and telling your story can be profound. More than once I've witnessed a child shyly reveal her deepest, darkest secret—one that she's been holding on to and afraid to talk about because of what she thinks it says about her—only to have another child across the circle say, "Oh, yeah, I've felt that way, too." The relief kids feel when they share their stories, and other kids relate to them, can be freeing to the kids and inspiring to the rest of us.

Actions Have Consequences

Sitting in a circle and talking with kids is a good place to reinforce the fact that actions have consequences. This simple and direct truth is known, in the vernacular of mindfulness, as the law of karma. Most children and teens have a practical understanding of karma that rivals that of contemplatives. They understand that the unfriendly words they use to describe someone, or the corner they cut when studying for an exam or writing a research paper, will more likely than not will come back to haunt them. They also understand that sometimes the consequences of an action or a series of events are not predictable. A classical story of a farmer and his son illustrates this point beautifully.

FABLE: THE FARMER AND HIS SON

There once was an old man who lived with his son on a farm near a tiny village. One day the farmer's horse ran away. The neighbors visited and told the farmer how sorry they were to hear of his bad luck. The farmer, a man of few words, said, "We'll see."

Lo and behold, the next day the horse came home and brought with it two beautiful wild horses. When the neighbors heard about the wild horses, they stopped by for another visit to tell the farmer, "How wonderful!" He again replied, "We'll see."

The following day, the farmer's son was thrown to the ground while riding one of the wild horses, and he broke his leg. The neighbors came back to express their sympathy, and again the farmer replied, "We'll see."

The next day, military officers came to the small village and drafted all the young men from the neighboring farms into the army—except for the farmer's son with a broken leg. When the neighbors congratulated the farmer on how well things had turned out for his son, they were met with a familiar reply: "We'll see."

Every action of body, speech, and mind has the power to bring about results both great and small. Kids can't control all of the consequences that result from their actions, and there are times when children (and adults) hurt other people in ways they could not have anticipated. But kids can work to understand better why they act in a certain way. If their motivation to act is mean-spirited, and they recognize it before they act, they have an opportunity to shift gears and do something else. In his audio series on the applications of mindfulness,[4] meditation teacher Joseph Goldstein highlights an "about to" moment, or the moment when the intention to act is set. Kids talk about having a funny feeling in the split second just before they do something that they later wish they hadn't done, maybe a tightening in their chests, or a sinking feeling in their stomachs. That funny feeling occurs in the "about to" moment. By noticing their funny feelings, kids can pause before they act to ask, Why am I *choosing* to do this? How does it make me *feel?* and Is my *motivation* friendly or unfriendly? If, upon reflection, the action doesn't feel right, they can choose to act differently.

It's not uncommon for kids to feel guilty when they realize that their motivations aren't always pure. This is one of the many times that the mutual support of a mindfulness circle can be comforting to kids. In the spirit of kindness and compassion, children can remind one another that everyone has negative feelings, and that it's perfectly normal to slip up and act on them sometimes. But through the support and encouragement of friends and family within the mindfulness circle, we can learn to act on them less and less frequently.

Personal character, intellect, and personality are developed in a fluid process, through repeated actions both large and small. Regardless of how much musical talent a child has, the development of that talent requires practice. The same is true with the cultivation of positive social and personal values. A child's true nature is kind, compassionate, and patient, and practicing those positive qualities will make them stronger. When children are kind to their friends, they are practicing kindness; when they are patient while waiting their turn, they are practicing patience; when they tell the truth, they are practicing honesty. The "about to" moment just before children act is their opportunity to recognize what quality they're practicing and to ask themselves whether it will help them become the person they'd like to be: Are these qualities ones that are likely to lead them to happiness? This is the essence of character development.

Antidotes to Sadness

My dad died on the Friday before Thanksgiving. The next day, Seth, Allegra, Gabe, and I flew from our home in Los Angeles to my dad's home in the Lower Peninsula of Michigan for his visitation on Sunday, his funeral on Monday, and his burial Tuesday afternoon. The cemetery was six hundred miles from the church, so, right after the funeral, we packed the car and drove for eleven hours to the Upper Peninsula of Michigan. I had been dreading this ride my whole adult life.

My dad had bought a minivan before his health turned so that he could take his grandchildren on camping trips. He never got to take those trips, but that day eating sandwiches and singing my dad's favorite songs, I was grateful to have the van because it made for a very comfortable ride. Over the course of the long ride, we cried and laughed together, and I felt grateful that since my dad had had to die, he did it just before a holiday weekend so the kids didn't have to take much time off from school, and Seth and I didn't have to take much time off from work. My dad was a highway engineer, and he had the most extraordinary work ethic of anyone I have ever met. I couldn't help but wonder if he had planned his death to be at a convenient time. I felt grateful for the work ethic and pragmatism that he had instilled in me.

The next morning was the burial service, and the minister, whom I'd never met before, prayed with us and for my father. But instead of being overcome by tears, I found myself holding back laughter as the minister repeatedly called us by the wrong names and spoke the words "Thank you, Lord" in an arrhythmic cadence. Biting my cheeks to keep from laughing, I saw that Seth was also choking back laughter. I hoped this kind minister thought we were crying rather than laughing.

Exhausted, we all left for the cemetery as the snow began to fall. A dozen strangers had formed a military honor guard for my dad, who was a World War II veteran. As the service progressed, the weather worsened, and when the military honor guard and firing squad began their tributes, the snow was falling so hard I could barely see. But I could hear them shoot volleys over Dad's grave as the haunting notes of "Taps" played in the distance. I was grateful for these patriots, none of whom we had met before, nor would likely meet again, who came out on a cold, wet holiday afternoon to honor my dad.

My dad died after a long struggle with Parkinson's disease. The quality of his life just before he passed away was diminished, and many, many people told me that it was a blessing Dad passed away. They told me that I should be relieved, but although I knew they meant well, their sentiments were not helping me or my family. But their actions were. It was tough to feel anything but misery, but gratitude swept over me during the small moments of connection with my family and with those who were supporting us. Through different ways and different perspectives, people have found a glimpse of psychological freedom by appreciating the small moments of happiness throughout the day.

Years ago one of my meditation teachers, Yvonne Rand, taught me a mindfulness practice to soothe sadness. It helps people view their life experience more as a glass that's half full than as one that is half empty. I still practice it today on my own and with kids. When something bad happens or when I just feel lousy, the practice is to acknowledge it right away (This broken dishwasher is a complete and total drag) and then quickly give thanks for three things. Any three things at all. The key to this practice is in its immediacy. I don't analyze what I'm happy about, or what I should be happy about; I just say thank you for the first three things that come to mind. Right now, as I write, I am grateful for Seth, who is sleeping on the couch in the living room; for the roses that are blooming in the yard; and for the fact that Gabe really likes his new role in the school play. And, because I cannot in good conscience exclude Allegra from any list of things that make me happy, I'll add a fourth: I am deeply grateful for her wise advice regarding my wardrobe. My daughter's sense of style is far more refined than mine ever was or ever will be.

Being thankful for three things is a small thing to do that could have significant emotional and health benefits. A number of experiments have demonstrated that recognizing that things could be worse can make someone more satisfied with the way things are. In their book *The Art of Happiness,* His Holiness the Dalai Lama and Dr. Howard C. Cutler cite a study from the University of Wisconsin Milwaukee, where participants were asked to rate the quality of their lives before seeing photos of harsh living conditions and afterward. Not surprisingly, the participants felt more satisfied after seeing the harsh photos.[5] The purpose of these practices is not to brainwash yourself into believing that life's difficulties are unimportant or don't exist, but to give appropriate weight to both the pleasant and the unpleasant things in your life. This practice just scratches the surface of mindfulness practices that cultivate positive emotions, but it's not a bad place to start, especially when practicing with kids.

Another classical practice that's an antidote to sadness is to reflect on the series of fortunate events that led to your birth. This practice can be a little heady for kids, and asking teenagers to reflect on the circumstances leading to their births doesn't always lead to the type of discussion we hope to spark, but the reflection can be framed in a way to be meaningful to kids of all ages. It's similar to saying before meals a prayer of thanksgiving or grace that considers the food's journey to the table and acknowledges all the people, places, and things that were involved. Reflecting on these details, like reflecting on the cycle of events that led to your reading this book, makes the somewhat abstract idea that *we're thankful for something* more concrete. It also reminds children that each of us is connected to many, many people, places, and things in ways that are not always obvious.

Saying thank you and writing thank-you notes are meaningful practices through which children can see the positive impact of simple acts of kindness on other people and on themselves. You can ask your children to write notes or send a package to someone who has been kind to them in the past. Perhaps the package contains a letter, drawings, pictures, collages, baked goods, or whatever your children enjoy making that represents a genuine expression of gratitude. They can mail it or they can deliver the package themselves and experience firsthand how good it feels to make someone happier with a simple act of kindness.

It's fantastic for kids to cheer someone up on purpose, but they can also make a difference in other people's lives without even trying. I once taught at a school with a grassy courtyard surrounded by a sidewalk. It was a perfect place to practice Slow and Silent Walking. One morning, while the kids and I were walking in the courtyard, I noticed a retired nun dressed in an old-fashioned habit walking along the sidewalk on the perimeter of the courtyard. I hadn't seen a nun wearing a habit like that since I was growing up in the Midwest, but I remembered that a few retired nuns lived next door to the school. The next week the nun went walking again, but this time with a friend. They were practicing their own walking meditation on the sidewalk as we practiced Slow and Silent Walking on the grass. Their presence enhanced our sense of community, even though each of us walked on our own. Walking along the outside of the courtyard, they held the space for those of us who were walking inside. Later, one of the nuns told me they looked forward to their walking meditation with the children all week long. Spending time with the children freed them from their ordinary routine and was a welcome respite.

Accentuate the Positive

I like the music of Johnny Mercer, who, together with Harold Arlen, wrote a song called "Accentuate the Positive." The lyrics go like this: *You've got to accentuate the positive, eliminate the negative.*

There was no scientific research about positive psychology at the time, but Mercer and Arlen intuitively knew that focusing on the good things in life could help people shift from a negative mind-set to a more positive one. There are many ways to accentuate the positive, but a fun and colorful one is to decorate your home or class-room with friendly wishes and gratitude chains, or for young children to make and give them away as gifts.

Friendly wishes chains and gratitude chains are easy to make, even for preschool-aged children. All you need is colorful construc-tion paper, a glue stick, scissors, and a pencil, pen, or marker. First, cut strips of construction paper and place them in a basket. Then ask the children to write either a friendly wish, or something they're grateful for, on one or more of the colorful strips of paper. If they can't write on their own quite yet, you can write the friendly wishes for them, and they can decorate the strips of paper with stickers, glitter, or markers. Each strip is one link in the friendly wishes or gratitude chain. Fasten the links together with a glue stick, and you have a colorful chain to drape across doorways and windows to dec-orate your home or classroom.

You can make a friendly wish or gratitude chain in just one sitting, or over a period of time. You can also personalize them for other people. Maybe your children would like to write down wishes for their grandparents and send a friendly wishes chain to them.

Eliminate the Negative

The flip side of accentuating the positive is eliminating the nega-tive. A lively way to do so with older children, teens, and adults is to write negative qualities that you'd like to be rid of on strips of paper and burn them in the fireplace.

Our family has a New Year's Eve ritual where we burn all the negative qualities that we wish we didn't have. We make a big fire in our fireplace, take out some paper and pencils, and everyone writes on scraps of paper the negative qualities that have gotten in the way of our being happy over the past year. Like pride, frustra-tion, anger, impatience, or anything. Then we put all the scraps of paper into a basket on the table. One by one we take turns pulling a piece of paper out of the basket, reading it out loud, and hurling it into the fire. Often the same quality appears in the basket many times because more than one of us wants to be rid of it. It feels great to start each new year having set the intention to purge ourselves of negative qualities, mental states, and emotions, knowing we have the support of the people to whom we are closest.

Chapter 8

Tuning In to Other People:

Develop Parent/Child Attunement

I wish to make my grandma happy,
I wish to get along with my family members
I wish to be cared for
I wish to be happy myself
May my wishes come true.

Middle-school student

Kids who think outside the box may be the most challenging ones to raise, but they can also be the most rewarding. Great thinkers like Madame Curie, Einstein, and Picasso were all once kids who thought a little differently. Galileo probably wouldn't have been the easiest boy to teach in fifth-grade science class.

Here's a story: a fifth grader at a progressive school was taking an art class with a substitute teacher. The kids in the class were painting with watercolors, and this boy was happily painting away—until his teacher looked at his work and told him he was "using too much green." This reminds me of the scene in the movie *Amadeus* in which the emperor hears a Mozart composition for the first time and proclaims, "Too many notes!" Duly chastened, the young artist finished the excessively green painting, and the class gathered to discuss the day's results. The teacher held up a painting by one of the boy's classmates that featured a human figure with hands in the air. She asked the kids what they thought the person was reaching for. One child said the sky, another said the stars, and another said the figure was reaching for her dreams. But the boy who painted with a lot of green said, "He's reaching for a sandwich." All the kids laughed, and the substitute teacher sent the boy to the principal's office. The boy walked to the principal's office worried about the lecture that was coming, but the principal of the school, true to the mission of progressive education, took the side of the young artist who had used too much green. Why wouldn't that figure be reaching for a sandwich?

The sky, stars, and dreams are clichés in this context. The boy who said the figure was reaching for a sandwich had said something that may have been accurate (and since that is how he saw it, it was certainly accurate to him) and also had the virtue of complete originality. This boy thought outside the box, and the substitute teacher's wholly inappropriate reaction was to become angry.

A kid like this can be challenging to raise or teach, but can also help his parents and teachers see things in a new way.

Out-of-the-box thinkers like this boy often have remarkable abilities to see experiences clearly, and it's wonderful when they are comfortable enough to speak up and tell us what they see. But that doesn't mean their perspective is always in agreement with what their family members see, or with the perspective of their classroom teachers, coaches, bosses, or other authority figures. Clearly seeing that someone, especially an authority figure, doesn't "get you" isn't always easy. Nor is it easy to understand that just because people don't get you doesn't mean that they don't like you. But understanding that everyone may not see the world as you do is a life skill that is especially important for out-of-the-box thinkers. It's also crucial for their parents, teachers, and the other adults with whom they work. Out-of-the-box thinkers are my favorite kids to work with, but I would be less than honest if I said that they don't get on my nerves sometimes. As funny, creative, and talented as these children and teenagers can be, there are times when it's tough to see them clearheadedly. But even when children are challenging to be around, when you're able to see them clearly, and love them just as they are, your love can transform into compassion. And compassion makes everything a whole lot easier.

Practicing mindfulness of breathing can help parents see their own kids objectively, even when it's difficult to do so. The classical sequence directs practitioners to observe their own breath, body, and mind first before turning to practices where they observe other people and the outer manifestations of their bodies and minds. The key to classical practice is learning to observe both inner and outer experience without blending the two. In the family dynamic there are times when it's challenging to stay emotionally steady and separate yourself from your kids. By practicing breath awareness in the midst of challenging situations, parents can settle into an open and nonreactive mind-set before assessing and dealing with them.

This is consistent with the modern view that to be fully present and attuned to their children, parents must first be fully present and attuned to themselves. Connecting the ancient insights from classical training with modern insights from interpersonal neurobiology, child psychiatrist Dr. Daniel Siegel suggests that mindful awareness is a form of both inner and outer attunement, a process through which we form relationships with others and ourselves. "When we focus our attention in specific ways, we are activating the brain's circuitry. This activation can strengthen the synaptic linkages in those areas [of the brain]. Exploring the notion that mindfulness is a form of relationship with yourself, may involve not just attentional circuits but also social circuitry. . . ."

Tuning In

When parents focus their attention on the inner world of their children, they're developing a more attuned relationship with the children. Attunement between parents and children, self and other, is the fundamental way in which the brain activity of parents can directly influence the brain activity of their children. Dr. Siegel has an interest in mindfulness and its relationship to the neurobiology of attuned parent/child relationships. In his book *The Mindful Brain*[1] he describes attunement as a method of coregulation, in which the developing children use their parents' mental state to help organize their own. By paying close attention to their children, attuned parents can literally help their children's brains develop in a healthy way. Siegel explains that when parents and children are engaged in an attuned relationship, and the parents' mind state is well integrated, the parents' minds stimulates similar integration in the children's minds.[2]

Mindfulness practice promotes attunement with others through the careful observation of the outer manifestations of emotional and sensory experience. There are several mindfulness-based mirroring games that encourage heightened awareness of other people in a fun and playful way. Backward Follow the Leader is one of my favorites to play with parents and their kids.

Backward Follow the Leader

It was a beautiful spring day in Santa Monica, California, where I was teaching a family program in a local park. We took parents and children out into the yard for a game of Follow the Leader, but this time the rules were more challenging than the norm. In this version, the children don't know that there's a game going on and, regardless of the age of the children, they are *always* the leaders. The idea is that the parents, unbeknownst to the children, simply follow along with whatever the children choose to do, engaging in whatever conversation the children initiate, all at the children's pace. The plan is for the parents to become completely and totally tuned into their children's rhythm, interests, and activities.

On this particular morning, a type-A dad had put away his ever-present cell phone to sit with his son, who, like Ferdinand the bull, was enjoying the shade of an oak tree and communing with the grass while the other kids ran and played. The effort to inhabit his son's world caused this dad more stress than a high-stakes business meeting. Next, the boy gradually moved toward a rock where a snail was slowly and steadily making its way across the stippled surface—an activity that the boy's father would later joke seemed specifically designed to torment him. The dad reluctantly stood up and followed his son, only to squat next to him for what must have seemed like hours watching the snail. On the other side of the park, a Starbucks-fueled mom, her caffeine buzz already running low at ten a.m., was darting back and forth following the flight path of an imaginary spaceship from *Star Wars*. Other parents were playing a board game with their daughter, sitting on their hands as they waited for what seemed to be *forever* as she contemplated her next move. Role reversals can bring about some surprising insights for parents into the nature of their children, how their children maneuver in their world and what it actually *feels like* to be them. And it can cause the parents to have an occasional insight into themselves.

The role of parents is usually that of corralling children's often wandering minds and bodies and shepherding them through a maze of goal-directed activities dictated by schoolwork, family, and community obligations—and sticking to tight schedules. Letting go of this role, the one in which you are a cross between an army general and a personal valet, and assuming one in which your children are in control, can be difficult, exhausting, and boring. *Boring* is a word many of us feel guilty about using in connection with our kids, but to be honest, following your children's lead can be very, very boring. Using the tools of mindfulness, we can transform these occasionally frustrating and dull moments into an entirely different, even interesting, and extremely satisfying experience.

The game that we were playing in the park is, in essence, a practice developed by child psychiatrist Dr. Stanley Greenspan called "floor time," which supports children's emotional development. In his book *Playground Politics,* Greenspan writes that the objective of floor time is to tune in to your children's world through spontaneous, unstructured talk or play and interact on their terms. Greenspan writes:

The idea behind floor time is to build a warm, trusting relationship in which shared attention, interaction, and communication is occurring on your child's terms. Floor time is the most effective way I have found to accomplish that goal. When that warm, trusting relationship has begun to blossom, you are laying the groundwork for tackling any and all challenges that your child faces.[3]

Floor time goes beyond quality time because the children, rather than the parents, determine the direction of the play or conversation, helping facilitate the development of an attuned relationship between parent and child.

Greenspan's floor time, and games like Backward Follow the Leader, provide parents with the opportunity to watch the activity of their own mind while engaged in a sometimes uncomfortable, sometimes delightful role reversal with their children. Siegel's work linking mindful awareness practice with attunement theory highlights the connection between mirroring activities and both a more attuned relationship between parent and child (interpersonal attunement) as well as a more attuned relationship between the parent and him- or herself (intrapersonal attunement).[4]

Watching kids mirror each other gives parents (and teachers) a good sense of their children and their interpersonal dynamics. Parents can get a sense of how children live in their bodies. Are they physically at ease? Coordinated? Well able to control their bodies? Because they generally require teamwork, mirroring games are also an opportunity for adults to observe the dynamic of the group as a whole. Who tends to lead? Who tends to follow? How cooperative are the students with one another? Are there one or more children who are often left out? Trying on Another Person's Movement is a game that quickly and playfully telegraphs a great deal of information to parents or teachers about their charges.

TRYING ON ANOTHER PERSON'S MOVEMENT

To prepare for this game, I designate an out-of-the-way place for kids to put their shoes so they don't trip over them once they start moving. When everyone has taken off their shoes and put them away, I ask the children to form a circle and choose a leader. The object is for the leader to move in a creative and playful way around the circle and for the others to "try on" or mimic the leader's movement and follow along. While the kids parade around the circle hopping, skipping, dancing, or jumping, tap out a rhythm on the drum that's similar in tone and feel to the way the leader is moving. When it's time for another student to lead the parade, you can signal the change by hitting the drum once, relatively loudly. When they hear the cue, students freeze and stop moving, waiting to see who'll be the next leader, whom you will choose by touching him or her on the head or shoulder. The new leader begins moving around the circle in a unique way. This sequence repeats until everyone has had a turn to lead.

Reflecting Back

To promote awareness of other people's experiences, I borrow elements from dance movement theory and theater games. Weaving those elements together with mindfulness practice has produced some of my students' favorite activities.

FUNHOUSE MIRRORS

In this game, children choose a partner, and each pair chooses a leader for the first round. They stand or sit face-to-face with hands held in front of their chests, palms forward and directly across from the palms of their partner's hands. The leader slowly moves, and the partner mirrors the movement. Both participants make sure to keep their palms as closely aligned as possible without touching; this allows them to experience moving in tandem with another person. Then the pair switches roles and repeats the activity. A fun way to modify the game is to have each pair take a turn in the center of the circle while those watching guess who the leader is. A third modification is for the children to form a circle and face center, then choose one child to lead while the rest mirror the leader's movement.

THE WAVE

While teaching second and fourth graders at Toluca Lake Elementary School, Annaka Harris adapted the classic Stadium Wave as a mindful mirroring exercise. With children sitting in a circle, the leader stands up and raises her hands above her head. As she lowers her arms and begins to sit back down, the next child is cued to continue the wave by standing up and raising his hands above his head. As one child lowers his or her arms and starts to sit, the neighboring child takes the cue to stand and wave until the wave has gone around the circle, once, maybe twice, maybe three times, all without anyone saying a word.

CALL AND REPEAT

The object of this game is to mimic the rhythmic beat of a drum without any verbal instruction. The leader taps a simple sequence on a bongo drum and then claps the same sequence out by hand. Without saying a word, he or she does it again, and before long, the children catch on and clap the sequence that the leader has just tapped or clapped. Once everyone has figured out how to play, the leader passes the drum to one of the children, who taps a sequence on the drum, followed by the rest of the group clapping it with their hands. The drum is passed between adults and children until everyone has had a turn to lead. You can vary this game with any combination of tapping, clapping, and stomping of feet.

BIG AND SMALL

Dance therapy and movement expert Dr. Suzi Tortora developed a fun sound mirroring game in which children mimic the rising and fading of a tone with their bodies. Everyone squats on the floor with bodies relaxed and tucked in like a ball. In this pose you wait and listen for the tone bar. When you hear it, you mimic the sound by stretching tall as the sound rises and squatting back down as the tone fades away. You can add voices to this mirroring practice, which I find especially effective when kids feel stir crazy from being inside too long. Kids whoop loudly and stretch tall when the tone bar is struck and grow quiet as they shrink back into a squat.

HOPPING GAME

The Hopping Game integrates mirroring with breath awareness and con-centration. Children make a choo-choo train by standing in a circle with each student facing the back of the next student in the circle. Place a cushion on the floor between each person in the train. Everyone stands in mountain pose and pays attention to the sensation of breathing. When the leader hits the drum, everyone hops over the cushion. The instructions go like this: "Stand, breathe, focus, hop" (say this at each beat of the drum). As children become more experienced, the leader can make the game progressively more difficult by omitting verbal instructions. The fewer the prompts, the faster the train moves. The prompts go from, "Stand, breathe, focus, hop" to "Breathe, focus, hop" to "Focus, hop" to "Hop," and ultimately, students are cued by one or more consecutive drumbeats. Before long, everyone is focusing and hopping without verbal prompts. The game deftly promotes awareness of other people. If a stu-dent doesn't pay attention to the other kids in the train, she will likely crash into the person in front of her, or the person behind will crash into her.

SHAKE IT UP

In this game, kids shake to the sound of a drum, trying to mirror the sound of the drumbeat with the movement of their bodies. Standing in mountain pose, children listen for the sound of the drum. When the leader taps on the drum, children shake their bodies, keeping the soles of their feet on the floor, their bodies relaxed, and their knees soft. Children stop shaking when the tapping stops. Look out for children who have a hard time toler-ating the sound of loud drumming. When playing with very young children, I start by having everyone pretend to put glue on the bottom of their feet. We then stick our feet to the floor (Stomp! Stomp!) and wiggle our knees while keeping the soles of our feet glued to the floor. To promote develop-ment of a sense of balance, this game can be modified by having children strike a balancing pose when the sound stops and hold it for as long as possible. Balancing poses range from standing on one foot, standing on your hands upside down, lying on your back with your feet in the air, and everything in between.

Jot It Down

Keeping a journal helps children and teens notice what they tend to think, do, and say, giving them an opportunity to reflect on motivation, actions, and their consequences. Journaling parallels the process kids and teens follow in a mindfulness circle where they meditate, talk about the experience to better understand it, and consider ways to apply what they learned to real-life situations. On a piece of paper, or in a writing journal, kids jot down their impressions after they meditate, making sure to describe the experience from the perspective of a friendly observer. Next they write about what the experience meant to them, considering their past experiences, future goals, and their sense of right and wrong. Meditation journals are not meant to be a homework assignment or another item on a teenager's already crowded to-do list. Much like sitting in a circle talking with other kids after meditating, journals are a tool that helps teens better understand their experiences practicing mindfulness by writing about them and seeing their process on paper. Make sure your kids know that their journals (or worksheets, if that is what they prefer) are private; these aren't for you to read. To give you an idea of what one might look like, though, here's a hypothetical example.

What I Noticed	Making Sense of It	Did I Learn Something of Value That I Would Like to Integrate
Too much to do	I always procrastinate	Don't procrastinate
I'm nervous and worried	If I procrastinate, I'll miss the party	When I get distracted, stop, breathe, and shift gears
I don't know if I can do it	I'll try	We'll see

Mindful Witnessing

Mindful witnessing formalizes the process through which we expand our field of awareness to include our own and other people's experiences without blending the two together. To witness mindfully, parents first observe and note their own experience from the perspective of a friendly observer. After checking their own thoughts, emotions, and sense impressions, they turn to the children and observe the outer manifestations of the children's experiences by observing not only what the children say and do, but also their tone of voice, facial expression, body language, and other nonverbal cues. Through this process parents heighten awareness of both their own and their children's outer and inner processes as they model mindfulness and lay the groundwork for healthy and attuned relationships.

The objective of witnessing is to build awareness of present-moment experience without reacting to it in an automatic or habitual way. The first element of mindful witnessing is self-observation with the intent to bring awareness to how your own reactions to experience (even those you don't act upon) may impact you, your children, and other people. The journal tracks the three elements—introspection, understanding, and applying what you learn to daily life—that I focus on when practicing mindful awareness with kids and families. You might make mental notes while watching your child playing on the playground with other children, or anytime that kids and teens interact with their friends or other family members. I don't suggest jotting your notes down in front of your children, but after they've gone to school or to bed and you have some time to yourself, here are some questions you might want to consider and use as a springboard for your witnessing journal. The aim is for you to journal what jumps out at you as you observe your children.

The friendly observer:

- Did anything they did or say trigger me?

- Did anything they did or say resonate with me?

- How did my body feel?

- What did I think?

- Did any emotions come up?

- Was I reactive?

Making connections:

- Are there any connections between what I observed and my past experience?

- Are there any connections between what I observed and my future goals, aspirations, expectations, or concerns?

- Is there any recurring theme or themes that come up in me with this child or class?

Applications:

- What would I do differently next time?

- What would I like to replicate?

Next, jot down what you noticed about your children's actions, relationships, tone of voice, body language, and other verbal or nonverbal cues. If you are a teacher working with a group, you need not journal about every student, but only those who stood out during that class. Here are some suggestions to watch for as a friendly observer.

- Nonverbal cues: Did the child appear calm, fidgety, bored, engaged?

- Verbal cues: Did the child say anything that struck a chord or resonated with you?

- Relationship with others?

- Were there any themes or possible habits that come up with this child?

- Overall impression of child's social emotional skills?

- Overall impression of child's attentional skills?

- Overall impression of child's self-control and reactivity?

- Overall impression of child's connection?

     With other children

     With his or her parent or classroom teacher

     With you

- Does the child have a sense of his or her body in space?

If you are a teacher, next consider the dynamics of the class as a whole, which may include the classroom teacher or another parent. If you are a parent, consider family dynamics and the dynamics between your child and his or her friends. Here are some questions to consider:

- Were there any qualities of this particular class that resonated with you?

- Were there any themes or behaviors that came up repeatedly?

- Overall impression of class's social emotional skills?

- Overall impression of class's attentional skills?

- Overall impression of class's reactivity and group dynamics?

- Overall impression of class's connection?

    With each other

    With you

    With classroom teacher(s) and/or parent

- Did the parent/teacher do or say anything that resonated with you?

- Does any theme or behavior come up repeatedly with this parent/teacher?

- Overall impression of parent/teacher's social emotional skills?

- Overall impression of parent/teacher's attentional skills?

- Overall impression of parent/teacher's reactivity?

- Overall impression of parent/teacher's level of connection?

    With students

    With you

Keeping a full witnessing journal after every mindfulness class or activity with your child is time consuming and often unrealistic. Jotting down mindful reflections on a worksheet from time to time is a useful alternative. Here's a sample worksheet that I have used.

What Happened Inside Me	What Happened Outside Him, Her, or Them	Both Together Me Plus Him, Her, or Them
Friendly observation	Friendly observation	Friendly observation

(continued)

What Happened Inside Me	What Happened Outside Him, Her, or Them	Both Together Me Plus Him, Her, or Them
Making connections	Making connections	Making connections
Applications	Applications	Applications

When keeping a witnessing journal and filling out worksheets, keep in mind the purpose of the exercise. It is a way to formalize the process of bringing awareness to your inner and outer experience. In other words, it is a way for you to clearly see and better understand how you respond to other people and how you respond to their relationships with one another. Ultimately, mindful witnessing is about you, the witness. It is not about the one being witnessed. This might seem counterintuitive, at first, but it is a crucial point. Unless the witness is clear about the purpose of his or her practice, the witnessing process can transform into a method by which parents and teachers judge their kids and each other, then create a to-do list of problem areas that the witness believes must be addressed. Not only is this likely to backfire on the witness if he or she tries to use these lists to get kids, teenagers, spouses, or partners to change, it is completely at odds with the aim of mindful witnessing.

Mindfulness Together: Viewing Difficult People as If They Were Once Your Child

No matter how compassionate we are, there will probably be people who bug us sometimes. So how do we handle that mindfully? A classical approach is to view everyone as if they have been your mother or your father. In the classical worldview, we all will be reborn again and again until we become enlightened; in this view, it's possible that in one of our many lives, every single person in the world was once our parent. So when you meet someone whom you find difficult, think of him or her as having been your mother or father in another lifetime. Compassion and love can naturally emerge from that visualization. When working with kids who are being difficult, it is also helpful to imagine that they are your own children. Somewhat miraculously, they may not seem less difficult, but you may feel more compassionate.

Chapter 9

E Pluribus Unum—
Out of Many Become One:
Live as Part of a Community

I wish there will be no terrorism
I wish that all the people in Pakistan and
Afghanistan are safe.
I wish that the police found Osama bin Laden
I wish the world was full of happiness
I wish there is more schools for the children
I wish everybody cared for all the people in
Pakistan and Afghanistan.

Middle-school student

The story of the daydreaming princess who lived long ago in a magical kingdom, about whom I wrote earlier in the book (Chapter 3), is based on a classical character. When we left off her teachers thought they could cure her daydreaming tendencies by asking her to give a lecture.[1] This gentle princess was very insightful. Floating on a bejeweled throne high above the courtyard at the Wisdom Academy, she spoke to the crowd of townspeople and students who had gathered on the lawn below. She told them that, in order to make the world a happier place, we must first imagine it to be kind and gentle, and then we can go out and make it happen.

Some of the students and townspeople didn't believe that just wishing people could be happy would possibly make a difference. But the daydreaming princess showed them that it could.

When I teach workshops for adults, I sometimes give participants a small, smooth rock, about the size of the palm of their hands, and encourage them to adorn it with meaningful words and pictures—words that represent the qualities they think will lead toward happiness, like love, fearlessness, compassion, kindness, joy, courage, patience, and equanimity. Once they've decorated their rocks, participants use them in games and activities throughout the day. Interspersed through the workshops are periods of introspection, instruction, discussion, and community building. By the end of the day, many are surprised that they've developed an emotional connection with their rocks, which often take on a meaning of their own. As a result, participants sometimes become attached to them.

A good chunk of the afternoon in these workshops is spent in silence, practicing introspection while sitting, walking, and lying down. The last section of the afternoon is dedicated to conversation, part of which revolves around a practice in generosity that points to what it feels like to give and receive.

Something happened in one of these workshops that reinforced the deep value of this practice. After lunch on a warm summer day, just before going into silence, we asked everyone to consider giving their rocks away during the silent period. We made sure participants knew that they were under no pressure to give away their rocks, nor any pressure to accept someone else's offering. Staying silent, participants could trade their rocks as many times as they were inspired to do so, or not trade them at all.

We sat indoors in silence and then practiced Slow and Silent Walking outdoors on the grass. Just before the bell signaling that it was time to come back inside, I saw one of the participants sitting on a chair in the hallway. I sensed he was reflecting on a difficult experience, processing a difficult emotion, or both, and I was moved to give him my focus rock. Not wanting to disturb his introspection, I placed my rock on the floor in front of his chair and walked away. I didn't stay long enough for him to give me his rock in return. The bell rang, and then it was time to start the Q & A session and to talk about the practice of giving and receiving. Some participants found it easy to give their rocks away, others found it difficult, but everyone who spoke found the practice meaningful. Participants were surprised by how many emotions showed up when they thought about giving this seemingly inconsequential rock away. Then the man I gave my rock to raised his hand.

He told us that he had thought long and hard before choosing the word *love* to write on his rock. Throughout the workshop he reflected on issues of love and betrayal, and on someone who had recently broken his heart in a deeply disturbing way. The rock took on a significance he hadn't anticipated, and so did the word he wrote on it. He was surprised when I suggested he give it away. During the silent period others offered him their rocks, but he didn't accept them. He wanted to keep his own. Refusing these offers of friendship made him feel uncomfortable, so he moved indoors, away from everyone else, to avoid another awkward situation. Then I showed up. He told the group that when he saw me, he clutched his rock. He didn't know what to do—he didn't want to give his rock away, but was worried about what I would think if he refused mine. While he was mulling over these feelings, I had come, given him my rock, and gone, without a clue what was going on in his mind.

After the workshop a group of us were talking, including the man struggling with love and betrayal. In the middle of our conversation, another participant came up to the man with the love rock and asked him for it. He cringed. I worried that this might not be the most skillful move on the part of the other participant, but I held my tongue, not wanting to get in the way of their process. The man reached into his pocket, pulled out his rock, and gave it to the other participant. In return she gave him a rock, on which she had written the word *love*.

A year or so later, the same man attended a different workshop that I was leading. I was delighted to see him and asked how things were going. He told me that trading his rock had been a turning point in his life, and that he now keeps the rock on his night table at home.

When Wishes Come True

Those who help children cope with chronic pain have long known that just wishing or imagining that you are happy, or well, or safe, or living in peace, can make a difference. Guided imagery allows children to shift their attention away from their real (and sometimes painful) life story to an imaginary one with a happy ending. By using the part of the brain that creates mental images or pictures, children's pain can shift. Their pain may not go away entirely, but consistent with what we see in other applications of mindfulness, the pain can fade into the background. In her book *Conquering Your Child's Chronic Pain*, Dr. Lonnie Zeltzer, a pediatrician who heads the UCLA pediatric pain clinic, explains that the effect of guided imagery and self-hypnosis is similar to the practical effect of pharmaceutical drugs like morphine or other opioids that are prescribed to treat pain.[2] When used with patients who struggle with chronic pain, guided imagery is a clinical application of storytelling.

Storytelling can be used effectively when practicing mindfulness with kids. There are stories that transcend time, place, language, and culture. Well-told tales serve to model positive social qualities that lead to healthy relationships, psychological freedom, and happiness. When practicing with your kids, remember to draw from fables and stories from your own childhood, and make up your own, too. This is an example of a story I tell that is loosely based on a tale from classical mindfulness.

THE FERRYMAN AND HIS SIX BOATS

Once I heard about a ferryman who paddled travelers across a set of dangerous and tumultuous rapids from one shore to the other so that they could look through a one-of-a-kind telescope. Through the lens of this extraordinary telescope, people could see the entire universe with pristine clarity. Few were intrepid enough to take the wild ride across this river, but those who did never saw the world in the same way again. Having seen life from an infinite perspective, even if only that once, their lives were changed forever.

Only six boats, with unusual names, were sturdy enough to survive these Class VI rapids. They were: *Generosity, Ethics, Patience, Perseverance, Concentration,* and *Wisdom.* But only the ferryman, who practiced mindfulness, could see clearly enough through the wind and the rain to navigate the turbulent whitewater and cross the river.

Here's another friendly wishes story, this one I spun from a tale my husband told Allegra and Gabe about an imaginary talking deer that lived in the woods behind our house.

THE TALKING DEER

Once I heard about a talking deer with a brightly colored backpack chock-full of friendly wishes. Every time that anyone, anywhere, wished something would come true, the talking deer found out about it and stuffed that wish into her backpack. The talking deer lived in the forest right behind our house, and one night, after Seth and I had gone to sleep, she stopped by and tapped on the kids' windowpane with her wet nose. Allegra woke up first. She then woke up Gabe, and in a flash they were ready to go.

Did I mention that the talking deer could fly?

With the kids on her back, the talking deer circled our house as Allegra and Gabe searched the backpack for the wishes to sprinkle over Seth and me as we slept. Every wish imaginable was inside, and they found just the right ones. After sprinkling friendly wishes over our house, Allegra, Gabe, and the talking deer set off to send personal wishes to everyone, everywhere. It was challenging to find the perfect wish for everyone on the planet, but they were up to the task. Friendly wishes rained down over schools, cities, states, countries, continents, oceans, lakes, rivers, streams, mountains, hills, and valleys until the whole earth was covered with them. Satisfied by a job well done, and with the sun peeking over the horizon, the talking deer flew her charges home and watched through the window as they climbed back into their beds. She was tired and ready for sleep, too. But before flying away, the talking deer reached into her pocket for the last handful of friendly wishes—the ones she had saved for Allegra and Gabe.

Friendly wishes stories are a form of guided imagery, and children love them. But they are not the only way to send friendly wishes.

WE MAKE FRIENDLY WISHES FLAGS . . .

Colorful prayer flags are hung outside of homes and in temples all over Tibet to carry messages of love, compassion, kindness, and peace to those who see them and beyond. The flags are fastened to the eaves of homes and temples, or they are sewn onto ropes that are then strung outside between trees. Each rope has five flags upon which are printed symbols that represent positive qualities—qualities that are developed by practicing mindfulness. The flags are yellow, green, red, white, and blue; each of the five colors represents one of five classical elements: earth, water, fire, wind, and sky. The wind is thought to carry the prayers of those who hang flags into the world, bringing everyone happiness, long life, and prosperity. It's easy to make flags at home with the sentiment of Tibetan prayer flags but without the religious connotation. Talk to your kids about the positive values that they'd like to see in the world and the friendly wishes they'd like to send to friends, relatives, pets, and other living beings. Use inexpensive cloth handkerchiefs and fabric paint, and ask your children to write words and draw pictures on the handkerchiefs that represent their hopes for all living things. Hang the homemade flags outside, and imagine that with each breeze, friendly wishes are carried from your home to people, places, and things all over the world.

WE MIME FRIENDLY WISHES . . .

Meditation teacher Trudy Goodman taught me this game, and we spent a wonderful morning playing superpower charades with a class of second graders at Toluca Lake Elementary School, in Toluca Lake, California. It was so much fun that I've played it countless times since. In this game, children can act out or mime friendly wishes as if they're superpowers. Students make decks of cards with pictures illustrating the superpowers they think are most impressive and would most like to have. On one side of a note card, they draw a picture, and on the other side, they write the name of the quality—maybe courage, thoughtfulness, patience, tolerance, kindness, enthusiasm, sensitivity, or appreciation. When the deck is made, we play a game of charades in which one student picks a card out of the deck and acts out the superpower while the other students guess what it is.

WE SPIN FRIENDLY WISHES . . .

Like Tibetan prayer flags, Mani wheels symbolically carry friendly wishes from those who spin them to others across the universe. Spinning the wheel is thought to inspire compassion in people throughout the world. In Tibet, special Mani wheels are constructed on land in places where they will catch the wind and be spun like windmills, and in rivers where they will catch the current and be spun like waterwheels. To use Mani wheels in a secular way, imagine that the qualities that are important to you and your family are imprinted on rolls of thin paper and wrapped around the axle of the Mani wheel. As you spin the wheel, imagine that you are spinning those qualities out into the world.

WE WRITE FRIENDLY WISHES POEMS . . .

When composing friendly wishes poems, there's no need for children to worry about rhyme, meter, structure, grammar, punctuation, and spelling. What's important is that their imagination is encouraged to run free. I've included friendly wishes poems that children have written over the years in mindfulness class at the beginning of each chapter. Here are three of my favorites.

> *I can meet my goals*
> *Brave*
> *Strong*
> *And determined to meet*

what I need
to overcome problems and failures.

I wish my life was always peaceful
I wish my life will be successful
I wish my sister will calm down
I wish I will always be safe
I wish my life will be full of excitement.

I wish that I can get easy homework
I wish I can have a lot of animals
I wish that I will never get in trouble.

When Wishes Aren't Enough—
The Importance of Community Service

My first thought upon seeing septuagenarian educator Dr. Paul Cummins was this: if a deep commitment to helping others makes you look as fit and trim as this guy, then sign me up. I was talking with him in his book-stuffed office at the New Visions Foundation in Santa Monica, California, about building character through community service when he told me the story of the Star Thrower by Loren Eiseley. Cummins leaned forward over his paper-strewn desk and told me about a poet who had been walking along the beach one morning at low tide. The poet saw thousands and thousands of starfish that had been stranded on the shore, baking in the sun. If they were left on the beach surely they would die. In the distance, he saw a boy sifting through the sand on the beach. The boy would stoop down, pick up a starfish, and throw it back into the sea. When the poet reached the boy, he said, "What are you doing? You can't save them all!" The boy knelt down, picked up another starfish, threw it into the ocean, and said, "I saved that one." And he did it again. "Saved that one." And again. One by one, until soon the poet joined the boy, and together they saved as many starfish as they could.[3]

That's how people who make a difference think and live. Bernie

Glassman, a community organizer in New York, voiced the same sentiment in a different way when he said, "I know there's no way to end homelessness, but I will devote my life to trying."

Dr. Cummins then shared a snatch of poetry from Robert Frost's "Birches" to illustrate his point:

> *Earth's the right place for love:*
> *I don't know where it's likely to get better.*

Cummins leaned back in his seat and looked at me, gauging the effect of his words. He said,

I don't think you teach character development intellectually—you can try, and that's a part of it—but it has to be more emotional and, if at all possible, experiential. Which is why community service—or community action—becomes so important. And as parents witness the growth that takes place in their children through community service, it reminds them what the hell education is all about. It's not all about SAT scores or which college you got into—it's about what kind of a human being has emerged out of this process who you're going to say good-bye to in the not-so-distant future and send off to college.

Dr. Cummins seemed wistful for a moment. As an educator, he has said good-bye to a lot of young people. He told me:

Kids feel that their future is dramatically diminished—when I grew up and stood at the ocean I looked out and I saw a limitless horizon. I look at it now and I see smog and I know that the ocean is filling up with plastic and garbage. At age twenty-five, my daughter came to me and said she's going to grad school in environmental studies. I told her that I have mixed feelings about that. I'm obviously proud of her, but I also feel a certain sadness, because I know she's going into a field where she'll experience nothing but heartbreak. She said, "Dad I know we're doomed, but I'm gonna do what I can." I thought, "My God, what a thing for a twenty-five-year-old to say. I know we're doomed as a species, and as a planet, but I'm gonna do what I can."

That's the value of community service. It gives you the feeling that you can do something, and, in fact, you can. And ironically my daughter feels less and less depressed the more she learns about how depressing the state of the planet actually is. Why? Because she sees places where she can have at least some impact. The problem with being a high school student, or a middle or an elementary school student, is that you don't think there's a single thing you can do about any of this. For kids with a social conscience, things look like they're just getting worse and worse, and yet here's another adult telling me how bad things are while trying to teach me about community service and environmental studies out of a textbook. What they are really teaching me about is human greed and rapacity and how human beings have screwed up this planet irredeemably and a lot of this can't be changed. . . . But by going out and studying the environment, my daughter is feeling like she's able to do something instead of sitting around and saying, "Gee, ain't it awful," and then becoming depressed.

Dr. Cummins paused and took a deep breath.

I got a bit off track here, but this is a long way of saying that action is the primary antidote to depression and alienation. Kids run the risk of becoming so depressed by the state of the world that they wind up being alienated from their own selves and everyone else, but when kids get active they see they can do something about it. [And when kids go out into the community and actually do something,] they almost invariably meet all these grassroots people working on interesting things, and they become heroes to the kids. They work in situations that are, on one hand, depressing, yet the work is inspiring, nonetheless, and so they feel as if they're doing something.

As I walked to my car, I thought about kids who have learning challenges and difficulty solving large problems because they lack the ability to break them down into smaller ones. They're like the starfish throwers in Dr. Cummin's story. There is no problem larger than the life of our planet. This problem seems insoluble, yet by breaking down a problem into small tasks, and making a difference at a local level, the larger and seemingly insoluble problems begin to be addressed. A child is less likely to feel alienated when she's changing the world one starfish at a time and he or she can start with small acts of kindness at home.

SECRET SANTA

In the classic holiday game Secret Santa, everyone writes his or her name on a strip of paper and places it in a hat or basket. Each person in the group takes a name from the hat and secretly gives a gift to the person whose name was randomly picked.

You can adapt Secret Santa as a mindfulness game to play at home, in a classroom, or with any group of children or teenagers. The object of the game is for everyone to do a good deed for the person whose name they picked out of the basket. The good deed can be as simple as giving someone a compliment, helping with a project, or drawing a picture. When playing with young children, ask them to tell you about their good deeds after they do them. Little kids will benefit from praise and acknowledgment. When playing with older kids, teens, and adults, the person doing the good deed can share it with the group but he or she doesn't have to. In this version, the beneficiary of the good deed might never know who helped her, or even that she was helped at all. With teenagers, especially, this can be the greatest gift one friend can give to another.

Civics

From the perspective of mindfulness, there's no greater confusion than the belief that we are separate from everyone else on the planet and from the planet itself. The antidote to this confusion is a visceral understanding of interconnection and interdependence. Once again it comes down to clear seeing. The motto found on the great seal of the United States says it all: *E Pluribus Unum:* Out of many become one.

Several of the games and activities in earlier chapters point children toward a visceral experience of interconnection. Mindfully eating a raisin, setting the ladybugs free, and giving thanks to all that's come before are just three of many practices that deepen children's understanding of this basic truth. As children learn to spot connections between people, places, and things for themselves, their understanding of other simple truths begins to unfold. They've seen for themselves the changing nature of life and have started to understand impermanence. They have learned to see life experience within a framework of actions and consequences, and they now feel the importance of kindness and compassion from the perspective of interdependence. As they begin to see clearly the connections between these simple truths and to recognize how they're woven through their own experience like silk strands through a tapestry, they are better able to understand how living things depend on one another.

Civics lessons come alive through community service and pack a visceral punch that no textbook or lecture could ever approach. Just as Dr. Cummins and the kind princess said, a true understanding of civics can best be reached when kids get out into the community and do something to help other people. Service learning is a new twist on this old idea that students need to do more than read about service and talk about community to incorporate these concepts into what they do and say. Service learning goes beyond the classroom and beyond fieldwork by integrating them into a single curriculum. To paraphrase the author J. B. Priestly, *it's not what is taught but what's emphasized*, and through service learning, rolling up your sleeves and getting to work is emphasized at school. Children best learn the importance of service by example. Community action at school is terrific, but there's no more powerful example than a parental figure.

Commitment to service and community underlies and quietly supports all mindfulness training and is fundamental to other contemplative traditions as well. The Dalai Lama has written many times and many ways that the path toward happiness and inner peace is through love, compassion, and happiness for the well-being of others.[4] Early research suggests that these qualities also promote happiness and well-being. Researcher Dr. Stephen Post has devoted his professional life to studying the connection between altruism and healing, and it's not surprising that his research, like the early mindfulness research, again supports what parents, families, communities, and contemplatives have long known through experience. In his extensive survey of research on altruism and health, Dr. Post wrote about the positive impact of altruistic motives and behavior of adolescents on their health and well-being in later life:

> Adolescent generativity (which is measured by three subscales: giving-ness; pro-social competence; and social perspective)[5] was related to all three measures of psychological health in late adulthood. Thus generative adolescents tended, more than fifty years later, to report feeling satisfied with life; being peaceful, happy and calm (i.e., having good mental health) and not being as depressed as older adults. Each of the three subscales [of generativity] were related positively to life satisfaction, but only pro-social competence and social perspective were correlated with mental health and only pro-social competence was related negatively to depression.[6]

To Arrive Back Where We Started

Community action during the complicated times we live in requires us to manage increasingly difficult outer experiences, and to do so we call on our own inner strength. In his book *Happiness,* Dr. Matthieu Ricard writes of studies that show "people who are best at controlling their emotions behave more selflessly than those that are very emotive." Much of the latter's effort when faced with a challenging situation is consumed by managing their own minds, which leaves them with less physical and mental energy to help others.[7] These studies serve as a gentle reminder that the path of service leads us back to introspection and the place where we began. Like a circle, it doesn't much matter whether it's service, science, emotional intelligence, health care, attention regulation, education, mental health, or simply the desire to help our kids that inspires us and draws us to practice mindful awareness with children and their families. Whatever the inspiration may be, it is just one of many ramps onto the same circular, high-speed highway. No one wrote of this more eloquently than T. S. Eliot in the *Four Quartets*:

> *We shall not cease from exploration*
> *And the end of all our exploring*
> *Will be to arrive where we started*
> *And know the place for the first time.*[8]

THE KIND AND GENTLE PRINCESS, CONTINUED

Back to the kind and gentle princess from Chapter 3, who spoke to a rapt crowd of students and townspeople from the Wisdom Academy's golden bejeweled throne. She taught them that everything, absolutely everything, is bigger than you think: your friends, your town, your country. The mountains, the seas, and the skies are all bigger. Everything is so big that we can never truly see the whole picture. But what we can see are the seams, the meeting points, the places where things connect. And it is by noticing those places, those areas where things come together, that we begin to develop an understanding of everything.

The kind princess spoke of all she learned while her teachers and the cool kids in school thought she was daydreaming. She reminded them that community service is important: "The Earth moves in a circle, the tide goes in and out, and the same sun shines down on all of us, so it makes sense to take good care of our planet and all those who live here."

Then she shared with the crowd an important secret, one even those who know about it often forget—that the secret to happiness is being kind to other people and to yourself: "By being kind and helping other people, you take care of yourself, and by taking care of and being kind to yourself, you help other people, too."

On the last day of her lecture, as she was sending friendly wishes, the most amazing thing happened. It turned out that during all the time that the gentle princess had spent daydreaming, she had developed superpowers. The kind princess lifted off her bejeweled throne and began to fly. After sharing the secret of happiness with all of her friends, and all the people in the magical kingdom, the daydreaming princess flew away. No one ever saw her again. But in my imagination, I see her flying through the indigo sky, night after night, pulling friendly wishes out of a big colorful backpack and releasing them into thin air just like the talking deer in our family story. Friendly wishes float down onto everyone at her school, her family, her friends, and all the people, and birds, and squirrels, and bugs, and all the living things in the whole wide world. May they be happy, may they be healthy, may they be safe, and may they live in peace with their families and those who they love.

In my imagination, as the kind and daydreaming princess's friendly wishes float down from the sky and across the world, those same friendly wishes fall down all over you and me.

Beyond This Place
There Be Dragons

May light always replace darkness
May love always conquer hate
May I get an A on my English paper
Even though its three days late.

Friendly wishes poem, Inner Kids
high school student

Centuries ago, mapmakers wrote, "Beyond this place there be dragons" to mark the spot beyond which they had yet to explore. For some it was the place where empirical knowledge stopped, and for others it was the place where adventure would begin. This phrase lost its relevance after all Earth's geography had been charted, at least on maps of the material world.

But the human mind is, in large part, still uncharted territory. In laboratories, and classrooms, and hospitals, and summer camps, and Sunday schools around the globe, a new expedition has begun. This time the explorers aren't carrying swords and fighting pirates. This time they are taking off their shoes and sitting cross-legged on the floor to meditate with children, teenagers, and their families. This new world is populated with babies, skinned knees, laughter, and spilled milk. It would probably have sent Long John Silver running back to his pirate ship.

Practicing mindful awareness with kids is still uncharted territory. I've done it long enough, and have been involved in enough early research, to have absolute faith that there are new worlds to be discovered. The journey is just beginning, and I hope you will come along. If you do, here's a suggested packing list:

> Find a friend to join you and watch your circle of mindful friends grow.
>
> Enlist other family members to join you, too.
>
> Find a native guide who knows the territory—in this case, a meditation teacher.
>
> Don't forget your maps! Here, your maps are the classical teachings of mindfulness.
>
> And most of all, keep your eye on the compass, which can be found by looking inward to discover the new world that's always been here.

Acknowledgments

It would be impossible to acknowledge everyone who has contributed to this book because it would mean quite literally everyone who has been part of my life for the past decade. A heart-felt thanks to all of you, but specifically:

My family: Seth, Allegra, and Gabe Greenland. My late parents Bette and Paul Kaiser; my sister Catey Bolton and her family; my late brother Bill Kaiser; my in-laws the late Rita Greenland, Leo Greenland and his wife Eileen Greenland.

My formal teachers: Ken McLeod, Ruth Gilbert, and Yvonne Rand.

My less formal teachers: Trudy Goodman, Suzi Tortora, Janaki Symon, Marjorie Schuman, Gay Macdonald, Sue Ballentine, and Paula Daschiel.

My greatest teachers: My students and children.

Those who have served on the Inner Kids Board and Advisory Board: Lisa Henson, Sue Smalley, Charles Stanford, Ken McLeod, Seth Greenland, Alan Wallace, Suzi Tortora, Adam Engle, Lonnie Zeltzer, Gay Macdonald, Paul Cummins, Jeffrey Schwartz, Daniel Siegel, Trudy Goodman, Theo Koffler, Jay Gordon, and Miles Braun.

Those with whom I've taught: Suzi Tortora, Trudy Goodman, Tom Nolan, Jeffrey Khoo, Tricia Lim, Diana Winston, Annaka Harris, Marv Belzer, Jenny Manriquez, Adrienne Levin, Gene Lushtak, Daniel Davis, Stephanie Meyers, Cathy Heller, Yaffa Lera, Susan Ladd, Peri Doslu, Jeane Pissano, Ellis Enlo, and Karen Eastman.

Those who made this book possible: my agent Susan Rabiner, my editor Leslie Meredith, and assistant editor Donna Loffredo.

I couldn't have done it without: Lisa Henson, and teachers, Steve Reidman, Dan Murphy, Jenny Manriquez, and Annaka Harris.

Researchers, inspired by practicing mindful awareness with kids, who were interested in the Inner Kids program: Sue Smalley, Lisa Flook, Michele Mietrus-Snyder, Jean Kristeller, Lonnie Zeltzer, Lidia Zylowska, Jenny Kitil, and Brian Galla.

Those who helped me with the book, through conversation or by reading early drafts: Seth Greenland (whose storytelling is woven throughout), Gil Fronsdale, Sumi Loudon, Annaka Harris, Alan Wallace, Gioconda Belli, Lisa Flook, Antoine Lutz, Daniel Siegel, Jeffrey Schwartz, Trudy Goodman, Marjorie Schuman, Michele Mietrus-Snyder, Jean Kristeller, Jack Kornfield, Jon Kabat-Zinn.

Working women who have and continue to support me beyond measure: It would be impossible to name them all but to name a few: Anna Mcdonnel, Judy Rothman Rofe, Lori Mozilo, Judy Meyers, Laurie Levit, Lauren White, Amy Spies-Gans, Nancy Kanter, Jane Wald, Alex Rockwell, Nancy Romano, Kristie Hubbaard, Melissa Bacharach, Leslie Glatter, Liz Dublemann, Carol Moss, Laura Baker, Jennifer Gray, and Mary Gwynn.

Notes

Introduction

1. For two excellent and accessible books on the classical teaching of mindfulness of in-and-out breathing, see Alan Wallace's *The Attention Revolution: Unlocking the Power of the Focused Mind* (Boston: Wisdom Publications, 2006), and Larry Rosenberg's *Breath by Breath* (Boston: Shambhala, 1999).
2. Nyanaponika Thera and Bhikku Bodhi, *Numerical Discourses of the Buddha: An Anthology of Suttas from the Aṅguttara Nikāya* (Walnut Creek, CA: AltaMira Press, 2000), 253.
3. Shortly after I began meditating with my own family, Jon Kabat-Zinn and his wife Myla Kabat-Zinn published a wonderful book about mindfulness and family life titled *Everyday Blessings: The Inner Work of Mindful Parenting* (New York: Hyperion, 1997).

Chapter 1

1. Jonah Lehrer, "Misreading the Mind." *L.A. Times,* January 20, 2008.
2. Carlos Castaneda, *The Teachings of Don Juan: A Yaqui Way of Knowledge* (New York: Washington Square, 1985), 82.
3. Rosenberg, *Breath by Breath,* 12.
4. Robert M. Sapolsky, *Why Zebras Don't Get Ulcers,* 3rd edition (New York: Holt, 2004), 10–15.
5. Ibid., 16.
6. Jack Kornfield, *The Wise Heart: A Guide to the Universal Teachings of Buddhist Psychology* (New York: Bantam, 2008), 49.

Chapter 2

1. Bill Moyers, *Healing and the Mind* (New York: Broadway Books, 1993), 128–29.
2. As in many ancient stories there are versions other than this one. This version is from the classic book on Tibetan Buddhism, Ratrul Rinpoche's *The Words of My Perfect Teacher,* new edition (Boston: Shambhala, 1998), 10–11. In another version of the story, told by Pena Chodron, the three defects are the full pot, the pot with a hole in it, and the pot with poison. The full pot represents the mind of a person who thinks he or she knows it all—there's no room for anything else. The pot with a hole in it represents a distracted mind, the same as the one discussed here. The pot with poison is the cynical, critical, and judgmental mind. Pena Chodron, *No Time to Lose* (Boston: Shambhala, 2007).
3. A Sept. 2007 study from the National Center on Addiction and Substance Abuse at Columbia University has found a correlation between teenage smok-

ing, drinking, and drug abuse (both prescription and illegal) and the number of times families eat dinner together during the week, with the largest impact being found on the youngest teens. Teens who have infrequent family dinners are three and a half times likelier on average to have abused prescription drugs; three and a half times likelier to have used illegal drugs other than marijuana; more than two and a half times likelier to have used tobacco; and one and a half times likelier to have drunk alcohol. Similar results were found with preteens (twelve- and thirteen-year-olds), where those who have infrequent family dinners are six time likelier to have used marijuana; more than four and a half times likelier to have used tobacco; and more than two and a half times likelier to have used alcohol. See Joseph Califano, *How to Raise a Drug-Free Kid* (New York: Simon & Schuster, 2009).

4. For an historical overview of children and play and how play serves as a means for a child's asserting autonomy, see Howard Chudacoff's comprehensive *Children at Play* (New York: New York University Press, 2007).

Chapter 3

1. Shunryu Suzuki, *Zen Mind, Beginner's Mind* (New York: Weatherhill, 1973).
2. Although I've taken many liberties with it, the story of the kind and gentle princess is based on Shantideva's classical teaching *A Guide to the Bodhisattva's Way of Life* (New Delhi: Library of Tibetan Works and Archives, 1979).
3. *The Vision of Dhamma: Buddhist Writings of Nyanaponika Thera (Vipassana Meditation and the Buddha's Teachings)* (Onalaska, WA: Pariyatti Publishing, 2000), 309, 323.
4. A more exact discussion of the proprioceptive and vestibular systems can be found in Suzi Tortora's *The Dancing Dialogue: Using the Communicative Power of Movement with Young Children* (Baltimore: Brookes Publishing, 2006), 114–5.
5. Al Chung-Liang Huang and Alan Watts, *Tao: The Watercourse Way* (New York: Pantheon, 1977).

Chapter 4

1. B. Alan Wallace and Bhikkhu Bodhi, "The Nature of Mindfulness and Its Role in Buddhist Meditation: A Correspondence between B. Alan Wallace and the Venerable Bhikkhu Bodhi." Unpublished manuscript, winter 2006, Santa Barbara Institute for Consciousness Studies, Santa Barbara, CA.
2. Jon Kabat-Zinn, *Full Catastrophe Living: Using the Wisdom of Your Body and Mind to Face Stress, Pain, and Illness* (New York: Delta, 1991), 33.
3. Maggie Jackson, *Distracted: The Erosion of Attention and the Coming Dark Age* (New York: Prometheus Books, 2008), 258.
4. Amir Raz and Jason Buhle, "Typologies of Attentional Networks," *Nature,* May 2006, 367–79.
5. Jackson, *Distracted,* 237–38.
6. Michael I. Posner and Mary Klevjord Rothbart, *Educating the Human Brain* (New York: American Psychological Association, 2006), 59–61.

7. Ibid., 210.

8. Ibid.

9. Kirk Warren Brown, Richard M. Ryan, and J. David Creswell, "Mindfulness: Theoretical Foundations and Evidence for Its Salutary Effects," *Psychological Inquiry: An International Journal for the Advancement of Psychological Theory* 18, no. 4 (2007).

10. B. Alan Wallace, *The Attention Revolution: Unlocking the Power of the Focused Mind* (Boston: Wisdom Publications, 2006), 6.

11. Ibid., 3.

12. Wallace, *Attention Revolution*, 13.

13. Ibid., 30–31.

14. Jeffrey M. Schwartz, *Brain Lock: Free Yourself from Obsessive-Compulsive Behavior* (New York: Harper Perennial, 1997).

15. Posner and Rothbart, *Educating the Human Brain*, 91.

16. Christine Alan Burke, "Mindfulness-Based Approaches with Children and Adolescents: A Preliminary Review of Current Research in an Emergent Field," *Journal of Child and Family Studies* (2009).

17. L. Flook, S. L. Smalley, M. J. Kitil, B. Galla, S. Kaiser-Greenland, J. Locke, E. Ishijima, and C. Kasari (in press). "Effects of Mindful Awareness Practices on Executive Functions in Elementary School Children," *Journal of Applied School Psychology.*

18. Ibid.

19. Ibid.

20. Susan Smalley, "Reframing ADHD in the Genomic Era," *Psychiatric Times* (2008), 74–78.

21. Flook et al., "Effect of Mindful Awareness," in press.

Chapter 5

1. S. R. Bishop, M. Lau, S. Shapiro, L. Carlson, N. D. Anderson, J. F. Carmody, et al., "Mindfulness: A Proposed Operational Definition," *Clinical Psychology: Science and Practice* 11 (2004), 230–41.

2. Wallace and Bodhi, "Nature of Mindfulness."

3. To learn more about Council, see Jack M. Zimmerman, *The Way of Council* (Las Vegas: Bramble Books, 1996).

4. Analayo, *Sattipatthana: The Direct Path to Realization* (Minneapolis: Windhorse Publications, 2004), 57.

5. Shauna Shapiro and Linda Carlson, *The Art and Science of Mindfulness: Integrating Mindfulness into Psychology and the Helping Professions* (Washington, DC: APA Books, 2009), 126.

Chapter 6

1. Shauna L. Shapiro and Linda E. Carlson, *The Art and Science of Mindfulness: Integrating Mindfulness into Psychology and the Helping Professions* (Washington, DC: American Psychological Association, 2009), 53, 65.

2. Personal correspondence, Michele Mietus-Snyder.

Chapter 7

1. Jeffrey M. Schwartz, *Dear Patrick: Life Is Tough—Here's Some Good Advice* (New York: Harper Perennial, 2003), 116.
2. Jack Zimmerman and Virginia Coyle, *The Way of Council* (Las Vegas: Bramble Books, 1996), 144.
3. Mark Brody, "Food-Rehabbing My Big Fat Brain" *The Committed Parent.* Posted online August 2, 2009. http://committedparent.wordpress.com/2009/08/02/ food-rehabbing- my-big-fat-brain/.
4. Joseph Goldstein, *Abiding in Mindfulness,* audio recording (Louisville, CO: Sounds True, 2007).
5. His Holiness the Dalai Lama and Howard C. Cutler, *The Art of Happiness: A Handbook for Living* (New York: Riverhead Books, 1998), 23.

Chapter 8

1. Daniel J. Siegel, *The Mindful Brain: Reflection and Attunement in the Cultivation of Well-being* (New York: W. W. Norton, 2007).
2. Dan Siegel's work is based on attachment research and the interplay of a specific type of brain activity known as mirror neurons. The topic of mirror neurons and healthy parent/child attachment is outside the scope of this book but is covered extensively in Siegel's *The Developing Mind* and *The Mindful Brain.*
3. Stanley I. Greenspan, *Playground Politics: Understanding the Emotional Life of the School-Age Child* (New York: Perseus Books, 1994), 26.
4. Siegel, *The Mindful Brain,* 697.

Chapter 9

1. For a lovely and accessible children's book about the life of Shantideva (upon which the story of the magical princess is based), see Dominique Townsend's *Santideva's Way of the Bodhisattva* (New York, Tibet House, 2009). And for a wonderful translation by Stephen Batchelor of Shantideva's teachings, see *A Guide to the Bodhisattva Way of Life.* (New Delhi: Library of Tibetan Works and Archives, 2007).
2. Lonnie K. Zeltzer and Christina Blackett Schlank, *Conquering Your Child's Chronic Pain: A Pediatrician's Guide for Reclaiming a Normal Childhood* (New York: Collins, 2005), 221.
3. The Star Thrower is an essay in a compilation of essays by Loren Eiseley. The details of the story are a little different than the way Paul recounted it, but the spirit of the Eiseley essay remains.
4. See His Holiness the Dalai Lama and Howard C. Cutler, *The Art of Happiness: a Handbook for Living* (New York: Riverhead Books, 1998); Clint Willis, *A Lifetime of Wisdom Essential Writings by and about the Dalai Lama* (Boston: Marlowe and Company, 2002); and Bstan-'dzin-rgya-mtsho, the Dalai Lama XIV, *An Open Heart: Practicing Compassion in Everyday Life* (Boston: Little, Brown, 2001).
5. The three subscales of the California Adult Q sort are givingness, prosocial competence, and social perspective. See Stephen G. Post, *Altruism and Health Perspectives from Empirical Research* (New York: Oxford University Press, 2007), 46.

6. Ibid., 46–49.

7. Matthieu Ricard, *Happiness: A Guide to Developing Life's Most Important Skill* (New York: Little, Brown, 2006), 208.

8. T. S. Eliot, *Complete Poems and Plays, 1909–1950* (San Diego: Harcourt Brace Jovanovich, 1952), 145.

Index

About the Author

Susan Kaiser Greenland developed the Inner Kids mindful awareness program for children and families. She teaches children, parents, and professionals around the world and consults with various organizations on teaching mindful awareness in an age-appropriate and secular manner. Susan was on the clinical team of the Pediatric Pain Clinic at UCLA's Mattel Children's Hospital for many years and was a co-investigator on a multiyear, multisite research study at UCLA's Mindful Awareness Research Center/Semel Institute on the impact of mindfulness in education and a collaborator on an investigation of mindful eating for children and their caregivers at UCSF. She also serves on the Garrison Institute's Initiative on Contemplation and Education Leadership Council, and as advisor to the UCLA Family Commons. In 2006, Kaiser Greenland was named a "Champion of Children" by First 5 LA, the largest and most influential children's advocacy group in Los Angeles. She has spoken at many institutes in the United States and abroad, has been quoted in *Boston Globe, Time Magazine for Kids, Better Homes and Gardens,* and *Publico* in Gutalajara, Mexico, and has written for the Huffington Post, Intent Blog, and elsewhere.

She and her husband cofounded the Inner Kids Foundation, which has brought mindful awareness to underserved schools and neighborhoods in Los Angeles since 2000. Inner Kids has been covered by *The New York Times, The Los Angeles Times, USA Today,* National Public Radio, various yoga journals, and *CBS Morning News.* She contributed a chapter on mindfulness and children to the *Clinical Handbook of Mindfulness,* published by Springer in 2008, and with her daughter started an online community for those interested in practicing mindful awareness with children, teens, and their families at www.mindfulnesstogether.com. Susan lives in Los Angeles with her husband, Seth Greenland, and their two children.